A REALTO[R]
FOR BOUNDLESS OP[...]

DOORS OPEN WHEN YOU KNOCK

STEVEN ROSS

Ignite Press
Fresno, CA

Published in the United States by Ignite Press.
IgnitePress.us

ISBN: 978-1-953655-04-2 (Amazon Print)
ISBN: 978-1-953655-05-9 (IngramSpark) PAPERBACK
ISBN: 978-1-953655-06-6 (IngramSpark) HARDCOVER
ISBN: 978-1-953655-07-3 (Ebook)

For bulk purchase and for booking, contact:

Steven Ross
Hello@DoorsOpenWhenYouKnock.com

Library of Congress Control Number: 2020921686

Cover design by Kathleen Cantwell
Edited by Emma Hatcher
Interior design by Jetlaunch Layout Services

To my three amigos: Evan, Zachary, and Sydney.

CONTENTS

FOREWORD

I began my real estate coaching career 27-plus years ago. I have personally coached more real estate agents on a one-on-one basis than any other person on planet Earth. For the past 15-plus years, I have had my thumb in Steven's back as a coaching client.

The thing you get paid most for in real estate is consistency. There are probably very few agents in the United States who have knocked on more doors than Steven. As a model of consistency and dedication to his practice, Steven is a real student of the game. He shows up every day, he pays attention, and he does the work. Everything that Steven shares in this book is based on real life experience. The good, the bad . . . the ups and downs, and everything in between. The business of real estate can certainly be a roller-coaster ride of emotion if you are not careful. Steven has learned how to tune out all the noise and distraction so he can stay focused on doing what is most important day after day.

The title of this book says it all—*Doors Open When You Knock.* YES THEY DO!! There are many paths that you can take as a real estate professional.

Most of these paths are nothing more than dark alleys that lead to nowhere. Real estate is not rocket science. It is a very simple and straightforward business. Only the clients and the deals are complicated. Steven is going to enlighten you on which paths to take that will give you the best chance to produce at the highest levels possible AND keep your sanity and well-being.

What follows is a roadmap, a formula for success, that anyone, no matter your background or experience or lack of experience, can follow. Steven is going to walk you through the process of what it takes to develop, sustain, and grow a successful real estate practice. For the next 100-plus pages, let him be your coach. Let him guide you step-by-step through the things that you need to do and master. . . and the mistakes and traps you can avoid. Steven is battle-tested. This book is not filled with hype and magic pills and false promises. This book details what this business is really about, the effort you must give on a daily basis, and the skill you must acquire through hard work, practice, and repetition.

More than anything, Steven really cares about you and your success in this business. He has been rewarded greatly by real estate. The pages that follow are Steven's gift to you so that you can build a business that is more predictable, more dependable, more productive, and ultimately more profitable. Learn from one of the best in the business and enjoy the journey of 100,000-plus doors knocked!!

Steve Shull
Performance Coaching

PREFACE

"Endurance is one of the most difficult
disciplines, but it is to the one who
endures that the final victory comes."
— Buddha

This book was written for me. This information is what ultimately guided me through the trials and tribulations of building a real estate business and becoming a real estate professional. Real estate is like a marathon. It is long, arduous, and filled with ups and downs. We don't need help on the ups—everyone can handle those. It's the downs, the troughs, that we need help in. When we are unclear, unfocused, concerned, paralyzed by fear, impatient, or stuck inside ourselves and our own head—when we are in those places is when we need the most help, and that is what this book is for.

This book is about picking a path and declaring that it is *the* path we will follow. That this path is the most important path, the one we are willing to give everything to. Oh, and the path will be hard.

As Les Brown said, "If you do what is easy, life will be hard. If you do what is hard, life will be easy." I ultimately had to accept that I am willing to do what is hard because success is not easy. There may be times when life (and real estate) is easy, but the times that are hard will be the real test. We will come to many doors on which we will be afraid to knock. Actually, we will be afraid to get out of the car and even more scared to head up the walkway that leads to the door—let alone knock on it—so we must develop the courage to walk and knock. To keep going even when there is no evidence that what we are doing is the right thing to do. We must stay definite in our purpose. We don't get off the roller coaster in mid-ride, nor do we get off the airplane until it has safely landed back on the ground. In building a real estate business it is the same thing: We don't get off in the middle, and we definitely don't get off in the beginning, when it's hard and unsteady. We only get off the ride when we have safely arrived.

We are going to talk about things that most of us probably know and have heard before. There is really nothing new here. We don't need anything new, we need to be reminded of the wisdom of timeless principles in exact moments, to keep us moving in the right direction.

I would never have made it in real estate, or have written this book, without the constant pushing and support of my longtime coach and mentor, Steve Shull. Steve has been coaching high-performing real estate agents for over 25 years, coaching the best of the best (www.PerformanceCoaching.com). He has been the voice in my head for so long that I can't tell anymore what thoughts are mine vs. what he has been "yelling" at me for so many years. From time to time I will refer to "Steve"—I am not referring to myself in the third person (which I would never do because (a) it's weird, and (b) my name is Steven). A large part of what is in this book has been my own training and development under his guidance.

We are going to talk about knocking on doors. Most people are not going to knock on doors. Some people, while reading this sentence, are going to put this book down because they think, "Knocking on doors doesn't apply to me!" Stop! This is *not* about you knocking on doors. The doors are a metaphor. You may knock on doors, or you may not. THAT IS NOT THE POINT! The point is that you will have your own journey. Yours will most likely look different from mine, and the way that you get to where you are going may involve very different circumstances. However, consider that the lessons learned are universal and timeless in nature, and therefore likely can apply to you as well. If you think that this book is about knocking on doors, then this is probably not the book for you.

A journey, by definition, requires us to stay in motion. For me, it's been walking and knocking. In ultramarathons they talk about "the chair." On those very long races, the desire to take a break and sit down—that is the kiss of death. Once you stop moving, once you sit down, it becomes very, very hard to get moving again. A worthwhile career in real estate is the same way. How do we keep ourselves moving forward? After all, in the end, this is a momentum business.

I am going to talk about some key lessons that we all need to learn—over and over. It is the *practicing* of these lessons that makes the difference, not reading and knowing them. The odds are that we will not get it right the first time. A decade and a half later, I am *still* practicing very hard to master some of these. I am clear that I will never "arrive." There is no place to "get to." No matter how much I practice, there is always some other element to master. I invite you to take on a similar approach.

We can't all be "number one." We can't all be "Rookie of the Year." If those are your goals—reading this book will be a waste of your time.

We all *can* be **our** best. We all can be great for the people in our lives. Remember, just because my clients think that "Steven is the best realtor" in their minds, does not mean everyone I meet will think so. That is the beauty—we can all be "the best" for our clients. You don't need to be the best for my clients, and vice versa. We could say that this book is about the journey to be our best for the people in our lives.

Who the heck am I to tell you how to be your best? I don't know you, you don't know me. I am not some real estate messiah. I have no special ordainment. In fact, you should be a little skeptical. Why in the world would you listen to me?

What I am saying is not "The Truth." Almost everything here I have learned from masters, whether they be in real estate or not. Some of those people I have learned from by working and training with, others by reading and studying from afar. However, everything in this book is what I have experienced.

This is not a "how to" book, filled with detailed instructions and action plans. Rather, this book is a guide. This is a place to come back to when you feel yourself veering off course. When you don't feel like taking action, flip through the chapters and see which one is calling out to you. Think of each chapter as a spoke on a wheel. Rereading that chapter is like fixing a spoke in your business. No one likes riding a bike that is out of balance, because that effort doesn't work well. This is to get you back on the road again, moving with grace and ease.

Let's get going.

1

HOW A REAL ESTATE PRACTICE WORKS

Before We Get Started

The point of this book is that there is nothing new to learn. What's missing most of the time for us is right action, applied consistently over time. To make the most of this book, I need to set up what type of real estate sales this content applies to. In other words, real estate is all-encompassing. This book is not for everyone and every situation. This book is designed for people who want to build a successful and profitable real estate practice. Not a mega team. Not an investment business. Not a discount business. An advisory practice. This chapter will lay it all out for you—so when you get to the end of this chapter,

> *What's missing most of the time for us is right action, applied consistently over time.*

you should know whether it's time to put this book down or to keep going.

A Few Real Estate Myths

You have probably read, seen, and heard dozens of myths, many of which contradict one another. I am sorry that I need to spotlight three more in order to properly set the context for this book.

MYTH #1: Your goal should be to make a million dollars.

At the time of this writing, a million dollars is still a really good income. While there is nothing wrong with making a million dollars, for many agents across the country, this is an extremely difficult proposition. For the agents that live in places like, say, San Francisco and the average sales price is $2MM and you sell 20 homes, making a million dollars isn't as hard. For most of us, that's not our world. I am also not knocking the people in high-priced cities who are able to make that kind of money—many of them are my friends. It is still hard, and by no means automatic, to produce at that level.

We will talk more about goals, and specifically your "why." The point here is that our industry throws the concept around that you *should* be making seven figures, and (a) there is something wrong with you if that isn't your goal, and (b) you are a total loser if you don't make seven figures.

MYTH #2: Whatever top producers say is gospel.

There is an utter fascination with "top producers." Especially in our modern era with podcasts, webinars, YouTube channels—access to so-called top producers is prevalent. The emails and social media ads for access to these mystic folks make it seem like they have some magic that will be imparted to you and transform your business overnight.

I have some bad news: that will never happen.

Do you know what all those top producers have in common? A winning mindset and working really hard. That's it. Do those two things, and you can produce at the same level (if you want to). I am not kidding. That's it.

Instead of being worried about what everyone else is doing, wondering if there is some secret tip you're missing—just stop. Focusing on what anyone else is doing, including top producers, takes the attention from the one area that needs the most attention: YOU. The only thing matters is *your* mindset and *your* action. Therefore, the thing to focus on is the process of improving *your* mindset, action, and skill.

Many top performers create great success without thinking much about how they got there, let alone imparting wisdom in a way that will make any *real* difference for the person listening. Furthermore, when interviewed, the information extrapolated by the interviewer is often not inside of a bigger context to move the listener forward in his/her business.

Before you completely blow your top on everything that I just said, remember that this is a general statement. There are always exceptions. I am not saying, "Don't ever listen to a top producer." What I am saying is that we **don't** need more content. *We need more applied instruction.*

We don't need more content. We need more applied instruction.

MYTH #3: Your goal should be to grow a big team.

This one goes along with the myth of why you "should" make $1 million a year. If your average sales price is under $300,000, the only way to get to a million dollars is to grow a team. In the early 2000s, one of Gary Keller's books, *The Millionaire Real Estate Agent,* documented the way to get to $1MM with a team, accelerating and spreading this concept and "should-be aspiration."

Here's why this is a terrible goal. First, many real estate agents don't have the skillset to run a team. Generally, most people who get into real estate do so to: *actually sell real estate.* Selling real estate and running a team are two different things, with two different skill sets. Running a team (and I mean more than three people, but this evaluation could also be applied to the agent and an assistant) is like running any other business. Running a *successful, profitable* business is ridiculously difficult. Said another way, it's friggin' hard. Many of us are not capable of doing it, and especially we are challenged to do it well.

Now, again, I am not saying that there is anything wrong with teams. The myth that I am busting is that we all should aspire to run a team of more than three people. For some people (and it's *not* most of us), growing and running a team is an excellent and amazing opportunity. For some people, being part of a team is fun and rewarding. Again, being on a team, or being your own solo practice, is not the same as running a team.

If you haven't been completely disillusioned yet on what I have said, let's talk about what *could* be a worthwhile goal in real estate.

Getting to Your Sweet Spot

What I am about to assert here is something that very few people talk about. In fact, most people will completely discount and/or ignore what I am about to say.

Consider that real estate is a low-volume/high-dollar business. Meaning, we aren't selling smartphone cases and we aren't selling dog grooming services, which are both relatively cheap (unless you have recently had your dog groomed for $100-plus—which does happen). We are advisors. We are fiduciaries to our clients in large-dollar real estate transactions. Large meaning six and seven figures, sometimes eight figures. We can get paid large sums of money for doing our job. We get paid *way* more than the groomer.

Sweet Spot

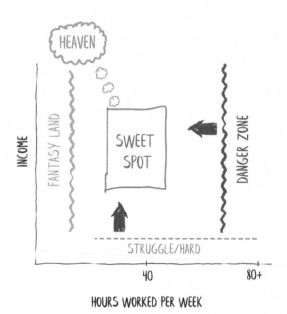

HOURS WORKED PER WEEK

So, would it be unreasonable to think that this is not just a "transaction-based" business? In other words, how many gurus and coaches talk about you growing your business to dozens and hundreds of transactions? Yet how can you advise your client appropriately as a fiduciary and also be out gunning for 100-plus transactions per year? Oh wait, and *not* work more than 30 or 40 hours per week?

The Sweet Spot diagram outlines the different places you may find yourself within your real estate practice. Along the bottom (*x* axis) are hours worked. Again, nothing wrong with working hard, but most of us at some point realize that working more hours is not the answer or path to the life that we are creating.

Along the left side (*y* axis) is Net Income, *not* Gross Commission Income (GCI). I am referring to the income that you receive *after* your brokerage takes its piece but *before* you account for your own business expenses. I have placed $150,000 in the middle, sort of a place to shoot for. In San Jose, 150K doesn't cover rent. For most of us across the country, $150,000 is a very nice income. For some, $100,000 is their goal, and for others, it's $300,000 or more. You can write in your own Sweet Spot income goal.

Let's go through each of the areas.

The Struggle

Ahhh, *The Struggle*. The Struggle is where most agents arrive in the business and hang out until they quit—or push through. The Struggle is hard. You are working long hours *and* not making any money. This is a *terrible* place to be. Most of us enter the business and find that this is what the first one to three years look like. It can take some time to get going. Some people are rock stars and are killing it from day one, however, keep in mind that they are a very small minority.

The Danger Zone

The Danger Zone is another place agents tend to hang out. The difference between The Danger Zone and The Struggle—agents can hang out here for much of their career because they are making money. This can be a trap for more seasoned agents who are addicted to working, doing deals, and the like. They don't want to miss anything—so they are always working. It's not about the money, some of them make over seven figures. It's called The Danger Zone because it is not a harmonious place to live. It's the place of working too hard, year after year, while not taking care of the other things in our lives: our physical fitness and well-being, our relationships, our creativity, our spirituality, and our own personal development and growth.

It is easy to justify staying here: "Hey, I am successful, I can do anything I want." Really? Can you? Can you take three weeks off without access to voice-mail and email? Do you have bags under your eyes? What is your overall health and physical fitness? How's your diet? Can you bend over and touch your toes? Can I drag you out of bed to do a four-hour hike? Do you have someone you cherish in your life and get to spend quality, uninterrupted time with him/her? Can you specify in what ways you have grown and developed over the last year?

I am not saying don't work hard, and I am not saying don't have large monetary goals. I am simply asking you to be honest with yourself if you find yourself in this zone and it's a trap that you didn't know you were in / weren't willing to acknowledge.

Fantasy Land

As the name suggests, there is no such thing as Fantasy Land. It *is* a fantasy. This area is what the public, and many new agents, think our lives are like. We work a couple hours a week making six figures. Sorry, haven't found anyone in this area.

Heaven (and the Next Best Thing to Heaven)

Heaven is real. We don't get to Heaven in our first year. We don't get there in year five or even year 10. Heaven is the place we get to after building a successful practice over time. We did the right things, day in, day out, year after year. Often we get to Heaven after 20 or more years in the business. This is where the phone magically rings with clients who love us, do what we tell them to do, and pay our fee. It's Heaven because we have systems, a really good assistant, and/or a partner who handles most of the heavy lifting.

Usually by now we are making very big six figures or more. Do some people get there sooner? Sure. Again, for most of us, this business was built over time. An oak tree often takes between 20 and 30 years to mature. Coincidentally, that's about the time it takes to produce a highly profitable advisory business.

What's the difference between "Heaven" and "Next Best Thing"? It seems like Heaven would be really hard to get to, and that it would take a long time to do so. Next Best Thing might happen sooner, maybe we aren't working 10 hours per week, but maybe 20 to 25 hours per week and still making a lot of money. Here's the point: If we do the right things up front, we have the ability to have a business that produces *a lot* of money without a lot of hard work. But—and this is a big *but*—it comes way out on the horizon.

The Sweet Spot

Which brings us to the Sweet Spot. This is the combination of *averaging* 40 hours (or less) per week, while making the six-figure income (or maybe more) that fits your goals and lifestyle. This is not about how many homes you sell or your GCI measured and evaluated in isolation. It is about looking at your income and how many hours you put in, and expenses you accrue, to attain that income. At the end of the day, your Sweet Spot is more about your *net* income per hour.

Maybe you have a goal of working hard, really hard, for five to 10 years and then retiring; then your Sweet Spot is a little different from others. However, for most agents the Sweet Spot is about maximizing their net income per hour, and increasing it over time. If you are familiar with Ninja Selling, created by Larry Kendall (www.NinjaSelling.com), then this is not a new concept. It's not about how many things we can do, it's about doing what's most important, operating on a schedule, and staying on track. Getting to your Sweet Spot is simply about keeping it simple: having good habits, practices, and standards that enable you earn a high income per hour. Here are some other qualities of agents who are in their Sweet Spot:

- They only work with amazing clients—bad clients waste our time and drain our energy.

- Charging a full fee and not not giving away our money in the middle of the transaction.
- Not spending significant amounts of money on lead generation (i.e., buying leads).

Doing the opposite of the above kills your time and profitability. The only way to make up lost profits is with volume, and doing more volume requires more time. Of course, you could hire help with the additional volume, but then that requires more expense. Doing "*more*" can be a trap.

Profitability Versus Complexity

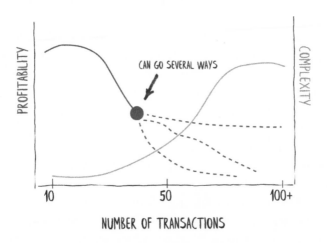

Profitability often goes down as number of transactions goes up.

Complexity of running the business and the transactions goes up as you get past 20 transactions (approximately). Getting to 50 and then 100+ require other sets of paradigms and operating structures.

Finally, if you are paying a lot for your leads, that is essentially the same as taking a reduced commission—or worse, you are taking a reduced commission on leads that you paid for!

Example w/ $7mm of Annual Sales	Commission Rate: 2.5%	Commission Rate: 3.0%
Gross Commission Income	$175,000	$210,000
Difference	($35,000)	

If your average commission is 2.5%, then you will make $35,000 less in the above example. That's almost $3K per month! In many parts of the country, this can cover the mortgage on a nice suburban home and maybe one car payment. We tend to throw around these numbers like it's no big deal, but $35,000 less (or more) for doing the same amount of work is a lot of money—the *annual* personal income in the United States is around $31,000 (2016). Reducing your fee to get business **costs you money**! It has a very real, negative impact on your financial results.

The point of having defined our Sweet Spot is that we have figured out what is ideal for us in terms of income and effort. Once we have defined a level of income that is desirable and attainable, it is not about doing more. As I said, doing more can become a trap.

I am also not saying that once you hit your ideal income goal you should sit back and cruise. What I am saying is that:

- Without defined goals, we never know what we are shooting for, whether it's too low or too high. Too low of a goal, and we aren't living our potential. Too high of a goal, and we are caught in the never ending trap of "more"—or "not enough."
- There is **no** guarantee of tomorrow. Today can always be our last day, or our last year, that we are on this planet. Therefore, sacrificing everything else in our lives for some potential future that may never come—is that really a good bet? Or . . . is it possible that we can live *today*, and have it all count? Can we still run a profitable business that allows us the time to have a life outside our business? That is ultimately the point of defining your Sweet Spot.

A real estate sales business is about serving clients. Therefore, before we move on, we need to define underlying tenets of client relationships.

Levels of a Client Relationship

In *The Trusted Advisor*, the authors (David H. Maister, Charles H. Green, and Robert M. Galford) lay out four types of business transactions and relationships. I think of it more as a pyramid. In the figure below, I have adapted their model to a real estate practice.

Trusted Advisor Pyramid

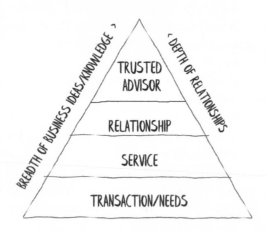

Transaction/Needs Based – This is the bottom of the pyramid because at the core, or foundation, there are some basic needs that must get met during a real estate transaction. These are the nuts and bolts of buying or selling a property. Typically, the people who only want this type of transaction can be, but certainly are not exclusively, those who go FSBO or flat fee. They are just looking for someone to help do the basic transactional work required to help buy or sell.

Service Based – Above and beyond the fundamentals of buying and selling, the next level of the pyramid is where customer service plays a part. This is where real estate teams excel: being able to provide an excellent service in the home-selling process. Of course, many solo agents deliver excellent customer service as well.

Relationship – At this level of the pyramid, people are doing business with someone because they are relying on their relationship with the agent/advisor to pull them through the transaction. It's not that the other two layers aren't involved (they are), but the driving force behind hiring that advisor was the relationship. This is where repeat and referral business kicks in.

Trusted Advisor – Not all transactions require this level of service—however, this is the pinnacle of having a repeat and referral business. When you become someone's trusted advisor, it's automatic that they come to you and refer you when they, or someone they know, needs help.

The first thing to point out: Not all transactions necessarily require the Relationship and Trusted Advisor levels. Most of us have been involved in a transaction where the client, whether it was someone we just met or a long time client, came to us for strictly one transaction. They knew what they were buying or selling, and they simply needed us to do some paperwork and handle a couple of items to get the transaction to the closing.

At the top half of the pyramid is when we have clients who come to us as their trusted advisor. It's more than just a transaction: They are dealing with something emotional and possibly complex. It could be that they don't know how to downsize or upsize, or they were recently divorced, or a death in the family is forcing the sale of a family home. Maybe there is tremendous financial strain. We have helped them through difficult or critical junctures of their life. It could be that in the past they came to us because they thought they had to sell a home in order to solve some other problem, whereby we showed them a way for them to do just the opposite: stay put and find a different solution to their problem.

What is critical to note: The further you move up the pyramid, the less you have to "sell" your clients. There is a level of trust and workability that often leads to transactions that are easy, fun, and profitable. Most sales and training systems ignore this point. They are telling you to convert everyone who is thinking about buying and selling. I am telling you the exact opposite: No one likes to be converted. Furthermore, that requires a lot of effort and is very expensive—both in time and money.

The beauty of getting to your Sweet Spot is maximizing your income while minimizing your effort (effort can be time and money). If you have a database of people who have a natural affinity for you and trust you, they will work with you, refer you, and *pay you your fee*.

Stop Here If This Isn't for You

Maybe you like to hustle, maybe you like to spend every waking minute grinding out deals, chasing people down. Maybe you love working long weekdays and sacrificing your weekends in the name of the grind. Maybe you prefer **no** time off because you are afraid you might miss a deal. And/or maybe you love the idea and power from running a team and all the overhead that comes with that gig. Or maybe you will not rest until you make your 10 million dollars. Well, this book is probably not for you.

On the other hand, maybe you have seen that the grind is not for you. Maybe you envision taking vacations—nice ones—and actually *being* on vacation, meaning, no phone calls, no email, no texts. You are checked out and taking time off. Maybe you want to buy a second home or investment property. Maybe you want to make sure that you have date nights with your significant other *and* not be interrupted with phone calls and texts about falsely urgent matters. Maybe you want to spend the time *and* money to grow yourself—whether it be on training within real estate or other personal development. It could be in taking time every morning to take care of yourself—meditate, exercise, journal, write, or paint—whatever it is that might fulfill your own inner spirit. And that followed by having downtime in the evening to get proper sleep so that you can wake up recharged, refreshed, and ready for the next day. If you are looking to simplify your business so that you can have a life, then this might be for you. This will not be about doing everything. This will only be focused on doing what matters most, doing it well, and learning how to do it over time. It really can be that simple.

2

WHY ARE YOU HERE?

We Operate Mostly by Default

Congratulations! You woke up today because you didn't die the night before!

Now what? What are you going to do today? Is your day a "*creation*"? Or are you just operating from what comes at you?

I am going to assert that most of us, when we wake up in the morning, just fall into our day. We have habits and patterns and routines that we haven't given much thought to. We wake up worried about what's ahead. We feel anxious about what we may have to deal with. We resist things that we know we should do but often don't feel like doing.

That may not be true about *your* day, or maybe not your entire day. Maybe you enjoy physical exercise, and you are lit up about something planned with your trainer or a friend. Or maybe you have a closing this day, and you are thrilled to get paid.

Personally, you have some special time planned with your spouse, or someone else special in your life. I am not talking about any of those things.

What I am referring to are the things that you do because they are in front of you. Yes, check your phone, your email, and any other messages you received. You (sometimes) call people back. You (often) avoid doing the things that are harder, more difficult, and take courage and inspiration. In other words, we spend most of our day *reacting* to what comes at us.

What are you doing today, and most importantly... *why?*

There has been much written, blogged, and streamed about asking people to get in touch with their *why*. Consider that most of us still ignore that question, spending little time thinking and answering it. I am not going to be one more person "telling you" that you should figure out your *why*.

What I am saying though is that, in the context of your real estate career, not having a *why* is likely going to be the first thing that keeps you from succeeding. I am not talking about some noble, all-encompassing purpose—although it could be. The question is: *What is going to drive you today, and the next day, when you have to do things that you don't want to do?* Or simply, you are having a bad day, that then turns into two, three, or 10 bad days in a row. When things are not going as planned, then what?

Real estate, like an endurance race, is peppered with moments when we are going to want to quit. In those moments, what are we going to do? In an

endurance race, people keep going. They pers
and finish the race.

What about all the people that signed up f○
the race but never showed up on race day? Or the
people that had a vision of their running a race and
never took action? Where are all *those* people? The
people who show up on race day are geared up physically *and emotionally* to finish (mostly). Consider
that many of us get taken out before we even get
started. Think about a time when you had an idea,
something that sounded cool and noble, something
that would be amazing if you did/accomplished it.
We have this flash of insight, and we are inspired:
Yes! I am going to do X! It will be AMAZING! I can
see it all clearly now! Yes! Yes! Yes!

We then wake up the next day, when it is time to
start implementing. What were we thinking when we
came up with that idea? Is it still a good idea? Now
it's sounding too hard. I will do it later. Or another
time. Probably never. And then, nothing happens.
Many of us have had an experience like that. The
inspiration came, followed by very little action until
the spark that started it all fizzled out. There has to
be some commitment that has us endure along the
way.

For many people, if they can see the finish line,
if they can taste the finish line, they are going to finish. But that's only the "20%" of the 80/20 rule. The
other 80% is made up of those people who had an
idea, an inkling of doing something, but then nothing happened. They had the idea, but never put it
into action. In real estate, roughly 80% of the pe○▪
don't make it. We could say that metapho○

are like the people who never really committed to show up at the start of the race, let alone trained, prepared, and committed to finishing.

Or . . . if you actually got started on that project or business or training for that race, then—then—you have to do the work. This is also where it can fall apart for us. The daily slog. The grind of doing the work, when things are not often fun nor easy. It can look like things aren't working, or it looks like no progress is being made. It is very easy to tell ourselves, to rationalize to ourselves, that we should do something else. In other words: we give up.

Why a *Why* Works

When I got into real estate, I did *not* want to go back to working for a company, or working in an office, or managing employees, or commuting. I didn't want to do any of that. I wanted to be in complete control of my business and my success. I wanted to control who I worked with (i.e., amazing clients, and **no** jerks). Most importantly, I wanted to be home to raise my kids. I wanted to sleep at home every night—no more traveling. I wanted to be attentive to their activities—I wanted to participate in their life. This is why I got into real estate.

When things got tough, I knew that real estate was my only option. I had nowhere else to go. I had to make this work.

All of the things that I wanted—being at home, no commute, and a flexible schedule—those were the things that told me I had to find a way to make this work. I had to find a way to get clients and help them buy and sell.

Now, those were my reasons. What are yours? Some people have financial or lifestyle goals. Some people have retirement goals. Some people have bucket list goals: like taking your family to Europe (or whatever your dream vacation might be). Those might be valid goals/*whys*.

Some people have no clear goals. Again, they get left to operating from default. Often times, they get left with no real articulated *why*, but some version of:

- I need to pay my bills.
- I like houses.
- I wasn't sure what else to do, real estate seemed easy.

These *whys* are a little better:

- I got into real estate because I wanted to have a business where I was in complete control and could be home (and in my community) to raise my family.
- I want to have a business where I work 30 hours a week and make six figures.
- I want to make [_____] dollars and support my family in this [_____] lifestyle AND be able to contribute [_____] dollars to a charity/church/organization every year (i.e., make a difference).

We are moving quickly here, and we are about to gloss over your *why* and move on. If you don't have one articulated, one gets filled in automatically. What gets filled in is usually something based in survival. Sometimes we work hard to have money so that we are never broke or poor again. Or we show everyone that "we can do it," and we literally nearly kill ourselves to be number one, or whatever other story we tell ourselves about what we're doing. It's impossible for me to have you stop right now and have you get the power of doing the work to determine your *why*. The only thing I can say is: you always have one, whether it is clear to you or not.

You always have one, whether it is clear to you or not.

Doing Things that Are Hard

You might be thinking, "Why do I have to have a *why?*"

Consider that your *why* is the answer to the question: *What is going to have you do the things you must do to succeed, but you will almost never feel like doing?* What is going to have you keep going when it looks like nothing is happening? *Whys* do not have to be grandiose or noble. In fact, I am a pretty self-centered and selfish person, or as my girlfriend says, "You have a very small orbit." My *why* had nothing to do with saving the world. *Your why* only has to be a reason that makes sense to *you!* The simplest place to look for the answer is: *What is your reason for continuing when things are hard?* Why are we focused on the hard stuff? Going back to the Les Brown quote, "If you do what is easy, life will be hard. If you do what is hard, life will be easy."

It does not matter which way we say it, but to get where we want to go:

1. We have to do things that are hard.
2. We are going to have to keep going when we feel like quitting.
3. We have to make both number one and number two above a habit—forever!

THIS IS THE BIGGEST TRUTH FACING US!

Knocking on doors is hard. Sitting in my house, a coffee shop, or the office—that is easy.

Going on appointments is easy. Getting out and talking to people to create appointments is hard.

It is hard to go up to someone's door and talk to them about real estate. It is hard to keep going when people aren't nice. It is hard to keep going when nothing is happening. It is hard to keep going when you talk to someone, they tell you that they aren't moving, and two weeks later someone else's sign goes up in their yard. It is hard when one of your friends buys a house without you. It is hard when the bank balance is shrinking and you aren't sure how your bills are going to get paid.

"Hard choices, easy life. Easy choices, hard life."
— *Jerzy Gregorek*

It is hard to run a marathon. What's harder than running the marathon? *Training* for the marathon. It is hard to run six days a week. It is hard to run after you have had a long day, and it's dark and cold out. It is hard to get up early and go do a tempo run. It is hard to go out on a Sunday morning when the temperature is 14 degrees, and your training schedule says that you have to do a 16-mile run, and your water bottles are already frozen at mile three.

However, the marathon becomes much easier when those training runs are behind you, when you had five months of good, solid training. When

What's harder than running the marathon? Training for the marathon.

you did every training run that you were supposed to, and you are prepared to run on race day, the race is *easy*. Although the race itself still takes something, it is easy compared to the five months of preparation. It really is. The real grind, the real challenge, was the training and all the things that came up along the way to take you off track. Consider real estate in the same way.

It's easy to go on showing appointments with motivated and qualified buyers. It's easy to go on listing appointments with sellers that must sell, and they want you to represent them. It's easy to collect a commission check.

NFL Hall of Fame linebacker Junior Seau said, "I get paid to practice. The games I play for free." In real estate, we get paid to prospect, negotiate, and problem solve. We get paid to go do all the hard work that leads to appointments and closings.

It's hard to do 100 open houses a year. Or go to 100 networking events. Or make 5,000 phone calls. Or knock on 10,000 doors in a year. It's hard to learn all the nuances of 18-page contracts, or the soft skills of keeping our clients calm through an emotional transaction.

When we wake up in the morning because we didn't die the night before, we have a choice to make. Are we going to do what is easy, or are we going to do what is hard?

EASY	HARD
<ul><li>Sleeping in</li><li>Grabbing for you phone and reading text or email messages</li><li>Scrolling through a social media feed</li><li>Watching YouTube videos—the noneducational ones.</li><li>Doing "stuff" around the house</li></ul>	<ul><li>Getting up early (before 6 a.m.)</li><li>Journaling, writing, and/or meditating</li><li>Reading books— lots of them</li><li>Exercising on a regular basis</li><li>Eating food that fuels and nourishes our body</li><li>Following a schedule that was made the night before</li></ul>

A Good *Why* Gives Us ONE Plan

Will Smith said, "If you have a Plan B, then it becomes Plan A."

We must have a *why*. We must also have no way out—we cannot have a Plan B. When it is time to do the hard stuff, if we have no *why* but we do have a Plan B—we're finished. We are guaranteed to do what is easy. And we are guaranteed to fail at Plan A.

As Smith said, having a Plan B is our way out. It becomes our Plan A. In real estate, Plan B shows up a couple of ways. The first is to go back to what we were doing. Maybe we were waiting tables. Or we were a freelance contractor/consultant. Or maybe we had a "regular job" that paid us every week, *with* benefits. Maybe it was unfulfilling, suffocating, and dreadful, but one that paid us on a regular basis. The stress of wondering when we are going to get paid, and how much we were going to get paid— that is very hard and very stressful. It's *much easier* to see the regularly scheduled direct deposit in our account every two weeks.

Larry Kendall famously tells the story of when he moved with his wife from Kansas to Fort Collins, Colorado. Right out of college, he wasn't sure what he wanted to do, so in the meantime he got a real estate license. Plan A was to do real estate for a while. Plan B never showed up. Plan A worked out very well for him. Now, is that the best Plan A? Who knows. **The point is to have one!**

When I got into real estate, I had just wrapped up four and a half years as a chief technology officer for a startup. It was a startup, which meant it was a little shaky. I usually got a paycheck—but not always. Before that, I was a consultant for Ernst & Young, where I did get a paycheck twice a month. A really nice one, with benefits. When I took the startup position, my wife was pregnant with our first child. When I got my real estate license five years later on March

15, 2005, my wife was eight months pregnant with our third child.

Here I was with three kids under the age of five, not getting a regular paycheck, and didn't have much cash in the bank. Really, all I had was the equity that we had built up in our house. Many people during the 2000's housing boom in Southern California used their newfound home equity as a piggy bank—and that is exactly what we did. We went through it **all** (feel free to judge me—just telling the truth about what happened).

Three kids to feed. Mortgage payment. Car payments. Nanny. Preschool. Lots of expenses, no paycheck.

That was scary.

Very big *why*.

It was either make this happen, or go back to getting a job in IT. The latter really wasn't an option because my technology and project management skills had weakened. Consulting jobs were in the toilet. I really had no choice.

No Plan B. Only Plan A.

Know what else was scary? Knocking on doors.

Doing Something Seemingly Crazy (But Good for You)

The first time that I went to knock on a door, I thought for sure that I was going to die. The noise and angst inside me were so loud, so uncomfortable. I was thinking, "There is no way I can do this." I first had to decide where to go. That took a few days.

Well, at least a day or two. I thought that I should just start in the area where I live, since I knew the real estate there. Okay, but there were 2,000 or so homes in the development. Which ones? Entry-level? Expensive? Right around my house, or farther away? What should I bring? What time should I go? What do I say? What if they yell at me and call the police?

I had to go. I had to do it. One afternoon, I finally drove my car down the street, hung a left, and drove another block. I almost could have walked there faster. I painstakingly sat in my car for another 15 minutes. I finally opened the door and got out. A late spring day in Newbury Park, California. Blue sky, 70-something degrees. Idyllic. I was terrified. My heart was beating so hard that I thought maybe it would pop out of me.

I walked to the first house and up to the door, took a deep breath, knocked—and waited. Actually, I prayed deeply that no one would be home, to relieve me from having to deal with the potential rejection and discouragement. Then a woman opened the door. I followed an old Mike Ferry script.

"Hi, my name is Steven Ross with Coldwell Banker. Would you like to sell your home?"

Taken aback, she paused, looked at this weirdo at her door, and said, "No." Then, she shut the door on me.

I walked back to my car and drove the quarter mile back home.

F*$k. This isn't going to work.

I needed a different approach. I remembered reading something Tom Hopkins did in the 1960s or '70s. He did a "community survey." He went around the neighborhood and asked people a few questions, tallied the results, and then went back around to deliver them. So, that is what I did. I came up with a few questions and started off. I went to about 1,500 homes, tallied the results, and went back to deliver them.

That was in the second half of 2005. It began my career in door knocking. I was still terrified every time I went to the doors. Worse, I was terrible at it. I mean really bad. The only thing that I had going for me: I didn't quit. I knew that I had to find a way to make it work.

I hated it, was terrible at it, but fortunately I somehow was lucky enough to believe that the action I was taking would work. I could get good enough that it would work out in the end. Yes, the doubt was still there, but I knew *why* I had to keep going: to have a business that allowed me to raise my kids. I knew what action I needed to take: knocking on doors. I had no Plan B—I had to make this work.

I built a sustainable business because I did what was hard. Over 15 years, 150 days per year, I got my butt into a car, drove into a neighborhood, got out of my car, and started knocking on doors. I never felt like it. I never wanted to do it. It was hard, but I did it anyway.

My *why* is what kept me going all those years.

3

THERE IS A UNIVERSAL FORCE HOLDING US BACK

Resistance

Maybe you know this, maybe you don't. There is a force that is working against us. Like gravity, but not gravity. Gravity's job is to keep us planted on Earth so that we don't go flying off the planet.

There is another force to keep us in place. It is called Resistance.

Stephen Pressfield, in *The War of Art*, defines Resistance as a universal force that has as its sole mission: "keep things as they are."

If you are not familiar with Pressfield and his writing, I invite you to pay close attention and see if this resonates with you. Resistance is the invisible hand that is grabbing the back of our shirt every time we want to take a step forward. Every time that we have a great idea that we go to implement, it is reaching out to pull us back down into our seat. When we are in a group of others and we have something to say, this is the force that keeps our hand from ever being raised. When we tell ourselves that we are going to lose ten pounds for swimsuit season, but wake up the next day and grab a muffin instead of a green apple. When it's time to make a phone call, this is the force that makes the telephone too heavy to lift. Want to know why stuff comes up when you are going to take on anything new or scary? Resistance.

To me, we can't beat something that we didn't know was there. So, the way to beat Resistance is to start by acknowledging its presence.

How Resistance Works

Its job is to keep us safe, like gravity. Safety is not the same thing as fulfillment. A plane has to deal with gravity the same way we have to deal with Resistance. A plane has a design and structure to it that allows it to leave the surface of Earth, cruise around, and come back down safely.

Similarly, if we want to "fly" and go places in our life, we must accept that we will have to deal with Resistance. A plane deals with different components of gravity. When taking off, the plane uses tremendous energy to get off the ground. The wings are pitched, with the use of flaps, in such a way as to create maximum lift. Once off the ground, the flaps are retracted, and power is slightly reduced. But not too much. At cruising altitude, power must still be applied. Navigation is important. Looking out for obstacles (i.e., weather, other planes, and terrain) is also important. Landing presents its own sets of challenges. Gravity is incessantly tugging at the plane, to bring it crashing back down. Speed must be reduced in order to safely land. Again, the wing flaps are pitched. Air brakes might be used. Gravity never goes away. It is always there, tugging at the plane.

Resistance is always with us—tugging, pulling, cajoling, pushing, yelling, bullying. It wants us to do things that are not good for us. We worry. We get overwhelmed. We beat ourselves up. We wear ourselves down. For me, real estate has been a graduate degree in Resistance. There has never been a moment where it hasn't been right there in my face.

In my experience, the two biggest manifestations of Resistance in real estate are: Fear and Distraction.

Fear

To be perfectly clear: I am a scaredy-cat. Most of my life has been spent "playing it safe." I don't like roller coasters (or at least the ones that do loop-the-loops), I don't bungee jump, nor am I much for zip lining. It is therefore not unfair to say that Fear has had me most of my life.

Fear is part of Resistance. What are we afraid of in real estate? Not making it, falling flat on our faces, people saying "no" to us. We are frightened of really going for it and not making it.

We are afraid of picking up the phone. We are afraid of working hard. We are afraid of what people might say or think about us. We are afraid of not being good enough, smart enough, pretty enough, funny enough. We are afraid of others not liking us. We are afraid people might be mad at us. We are afraid of mean people.

To avoid our fears, we make up stories to keep us safe. We do what is comfortable. We do what feels good.

Patrick Sweeney, author of *Fear Is Fuel*, says that "our dreams are on the other side of fear" and that "fear is the indicator of where we need to go." As I described in the previous chapter, door knocking seemed like absolutely the scariest thing in the world. I mean, what is sillier than knocking on a stranger's door and asking them about buying or selling a home? That is just about the dumbest thing that I can think of doing. It scared the living crap out of me for a good part of 15 years. I never ever wanted to go to the doors. The initial trepidation, the pit in my stomach that comes every time I drive into a neighborhood, get out of my car, and walk to the first door of the day—it has never gone away.

The translation to you is that if I can do it, so can you. If I can have the fear every day and still do it, so can you. As Franklin D. Roosevelt said, "Courage is not the absence of fear." Courage happens in the presence of Fear. Without Fear, there is no opportunity for courage.

Distraction

Distraction derails desire. Distractions are my other big enemy. Distraction is omnipresent and absolutely deadly to our dreams and goals; to say nothing of simply having peace and freedom in our daily lives.

The dictionary defines Distraction as:

- Lack of ability to pay attention;
- Lack of interest in the object of attention;
- *That which amuses, entertains, or diverts; amusement; entertainment;*
- *The great intensity, novelty or attractiveness of something other than the object of attention.*

I italicized the last two on purpose.

Distraction has many facets. At the highest level, Distraction keeps us from determining what is most important vs. what is urgent (we will talk more about this in the next chapter). Distraction is in the background, keeping us numb, not present, and preventing us from taking thoughtful, quiet time to really decide and commit to what's most important. This leaves us with what's in front of us, "the urgent." The urgent is all the inbound, everyday stuff that keeps us "busy" all day. Doing what's most important is much harder than attending to what's urgent.

But day to day, and moment to moment, distraction looks like:

- Phone calls
- Texts
- Social media
- Web surfing
- Television
- Music
- Netflix
- Hunger
- Thirst
- Bathroom
- "Play time"
- Clean the house
- Naps
- Laundry
- Spouse
- Kids
- Parents
- Life events
- "Urgencies" . . .
- Mis-prioritization
- Worry

And many, many more.

So, how does this apply to us and our real estate businesses? As an anti-social introvert [SR1], the last thing that I want to do is go out and talk to people. In the beginning of my real estate career, before I was knocking on doors, I thought that I would make phone calls. Here's is how it went:

- I need to find the perfect time to make the calls.
- I need to find the perfect place to make the calls.
- I need to go to the bathroom before I start.
- I am thirsty—let me get a glass of water before I start.
- Let me check my email before I make a call.

- Let me look up something about that person before I call.
- I have to use the bathroom again.
- Whoops—out of time. Have to make calls tomorrow.

What's underlying all these distractions and excuses? Fear. I don't want to make the calls because I am afraid of what people might say or how they might react. I am afraid of what people may say or think about me—that I might be rejected and/or humiliated. However, that's not necessarily how it shows up in the moment. In the moment, it shows up often as a distraction. Distraction, because it is a subset of Resistance, is also a force. Distraction is fulfilling on Resistance's purpose to keep me safe and the same. However, I need to feed my family, and I do that through selling real estate. The way to sell real estate is to talk to people. But I didn't "want" to talk to people. Of course, that wasn't me talking, it was Resistance. It had me thinking, "Why not spend money on marketing? Go to lots of classes and get ready to get ready. Spend lots of time preparing." Preparing for what? Preparing to prepare. To keep me out of actually doing. I could go online and find other people who built their business in comfortable, safe ways that did not threaten their identity. Why did I build my entire business on door knocking? It seemed like the only way that I was going to overcome Fear and Distraction. It was the only way that I was going to grow myself into the person who I needed to become.

How Door Knocking Put Me Head On with Resistance

Door knocking is the best lesson in Fear and Distraction. Knocking on doors is beautiful and elegant in its simplicity—of course, only after you get out of the car. As the old saying goes, "The toughest door to open is the car door."

As the old saying goes, "The toughest door to open is the car door."

Here are just a few of the things I found to stop us from getting to the doors:

- Where to go?
- What time to go?
- What to bring?
- What to wear?
- What to say?
- How long should we go for?

Now, each one of those questions could stop someone from actually knocking on doors for months . . . if ever. We can easily get caught up in all the minutiae that really does not matter:

- Where to go: Research neighborhoods for turnover rates, current activity, price points, types of people that live there, etc.
- What time to go: Search online for other people's experience. Go too late, and you risk upsetting people eating dinner. Go too early, and not enough people are home. If someone's not home, should you go back?

- Okay, well, what should I bring? A flyer? A fancy packet/pamphlet? Maybe we should bring a gift? How many? How will I carry everything? Which then leads me to: What should I wear? Should I be in business attire? What about shoes? If I am too formal, will I scare people off? What if I dress too casual?

- What the heck should I say? What is the perfect script? What happens if they are upset because I knocked on their door? Then what? How long do I have to go for? An hour? Thirty minutes? Two hours—no way! I can't walk that long!

Are you exhausted yet?

Do you get the insanity and inherent evilness of this force? It is out to get us!

Eventually I got into a rhythm: I knew where I was going, what time I was going, and what to wear, etc. However, for a long time I was still getting caught up on what to bring, if anything. Would I leave something at each door? How many could I carry, afford, etc.

I decided that I would bring a market update/newsletter. Or, if I was promoting a just-listed/just-sold, I could bring a specific flyer. In any case, I cannot tell you how many times I would make something to "bring and leave" at the door, print 100 of them, then drive from the office to where I would knock. I would get out of the car, look at what I had printed out, and realize: "*Oh s@#&?! There are typos on this! I can't use this!"* Then, I would drive back to the office, make the change, and reprint them. One and half hours later, I was ready. Of course, now it's "too late" to go to the doors. Or, if I did go, it was for a much shorter period of time. Either way: Resistance got me!

There are so many ways for Distraction and Resistance to get us! The previous paragraph was *one* scenario. I could have given you 10 different permutations of that situation. Here are few more. Imagine that we have everything ready. We're dressed and ready to go. We get in our car to drive to where we will door knock. Then:

- We get a phone call or text that upsets us.
- A client calls, urgently asking us to show a home in an hour and a half.
- An agent calls with an offer on one of our listings.
- A buyer client calls to tell us that they have changed their mind and want to cancel their purchase.
- On the way to where we are going we see a "coming soon" sign . . . on our friend's house!

OR . . .

- We go to check our email one more time before getting out of the car.
- We have to go to the bathroom . . . again. We could spend another 20 to 30 minutes

driving to a restroom, then back to where we need to park the car.

- We stop to do an errand on the way to where we need to be—thinking, "It's on the way."

OR...

- We tell a client we will "quickly" show them that one house before we knock.
- We agree to that "coffee" appointment with the lender/title/home warranty rep that wants to sell us on their services.
- We book a doctor/dentist/veterinarian appointment at 10 a.m., knowing that our door knocking appointment is at 11 . . . there is no way that we will make it on time . . . but we do it anyway.

All of these things are in the way. They are all forms of Resistance. They are all keeping us from doing what is most important.

Now, you might be thinking that door knocking seems like the worst activity to beat Resistance. Ah, but wait. Here comes the elegant part. Look at the following picture, what do you see?

People typically say, "Houses, trees, street, grass, etc." Those are all there. The question is more like, "What *don't* you see in that picture?" The answer is: NOTHING! There is NOTHING in that picture! By nothing, I mean: no food, no bathrooms, no phone, no texting, no computers, no internet, no shopping, no Netflix, no music, no laundry—there is *nothing* to distract me!!! Once I actually can get my butt out there, I am free! I have gotten to a place where there is nothing to stop me. *That* is my favorite part of door knocking. It gives me the experience of being present, in the moment, doing what I need to be doing to move my business forward.

Hey Steven—you said that this wasn't about door knocking! That's right, it's not. The key is to look at the example as a metaphor. You may not want to knock on doors, but how can you create a space where Resistance (and specifically Distraction) can't get you?

NOTE: Even as I edited these last few pages, Resistance was sky-high. I've found myself wanting to do something else—anything else—other than sitting down and reading what I had written, figuring out the best way to say it, and making sure that it made sense. I couldn't help but feel the constant urge to pick up my phone and check some random fact or piece of information with which my brain wanted to distract me. Colorado mountains just got three feet of snow... let's look at the webcams, check my calendar, when can I go skiing this week...?

Creating space and time, creating an environment that supports what we must accomplish, is critical. Otherwise, our chances for success are doomed. There are too many reasons, too much noise, so many external factors that can keep us where we are. Resistance will *always* be with us. There is always an opportunity to stop what we're doing and ask, "What's happening here? Am I in charge? Or is Resistance driving the car?"

As we proceed through this book, the thing to get is that, no matter what action we are talking about, we will always be dealing with Resistance— something that we are afraid of, something to be distracted by. Stephen Pressfield, who coined the term *Resistance*, has written several books on this topic—a good indication that it doesn't go away. Seth Godin calls it the "lizard brain" taking over. We cannot proceed effectively without acknowledging the forces against us. If I got nothing else out of my real estate career, it was the opportunity to see how Fear and Distraction are there in every moment of my life. They never go away. So, when I go to do something and I feel myself being pulled—either by the pit of nervousness in my stomach, or the urge to distract my attention, I am very clear what is happening in that moment. It is now not a mystery—I know what is happening when I give in to those fears and urges. It is always within my power to choose which way to proceed.

4

WINNING THE BATTLE
OF IMPORTANT
VS. URGENT

The Most Important Action in Real Estate

As Gary Keller says in *The ONE Thing*, the most important action is "the one thing" that makes everything else easier or unnecessary. In the case of our real estate businesses, for most agents the most important activity is talking to people. *How* we talk to people is up to the individual agent. However, in real estate we are constantly faced with urgent actions, which are not the same things as the most important actions. In the end, we must take important action consistently—and ignore everything else. This is so simple, so obvious, and seems so easy. But as you have probably experienced, it is extremely difficult to practice on a regular and consistent basis.

When I got into real estate, my coach, Steve, made it very clear to me: make your contacts. It would be fair to say that amongst the thousands of agents who worked with Steve, there was no misunderstanding his message. At some point, every one of them would say, "Stop yelling at us to make our contacts!" Now he wasn't really yelling at us, but to some people it felt that way. Nobody wanted to do the one thing that would absolutely make our business successful. What he was saying was to get in the habit of talking to people.

Here is the big disconnect: Agents start every year with a goal of making more sales and money— whether expressed separately or together. Agents then track their progress against this goal. How many sales have they made? How much money have they earned? Usually, the gap begins to grow between these two as the year goes along. Why?

There is no activity called "make sales," there is only an activity called "make contact." Making contact includes activities like phone calls, door knocking, open house, social networking, etc. People struggle with the idea of focusing on the *leading* activity. The time-tested nature of real estate follows this progression:

> Contacts = Leads,
> Leads = Appointments,
> Appointments = Contracts,
> Contracts = Closings.

Where does it all start? Making contacts!

Quick Review: The 80/20 Rule

In Gary Keller's book *The ONE Thing*, he eloquently demonstrates how Pareto's 80/20 principle applies to business and life. It is so important and critical that, even if you "know" this concept, it bears repeating.

Vilfredo Pareto was an Italian economist in the nineteenth century. He described Italy's income distribution as 80% of the land owned by 20% of the people, hence the 80/20 rule. You have likely heard that 20% of the realtors do 80% of the business. Conversely, 80% of our results come from 20% of our efforts.

Joseph M. Juran, a consultant for Western Electric in the 1930s, was brought into General Motors to solve an error with a card reading machine (any of you born after 1975 probably have no idea what that is—Google it). Working through the night, he solved the mystery. As a quality control expert, he began to notice that (as in this case) a few errors caused the majority of the defects, which he labeled as the "vital few, trivial many." That label wasn't sexy or sticky, so it became Pareto's Principle.

I was exposed to this principle long before I truly understood the history and depth of it. In the early 1990s, while I was finishing up college and looking for a "real" job, I worked for my dad's microfilm and document management business (which, by the way, *was* a real job). He and his key managers were trying to find how they could simplify their business and increase their profits. It finally dawned on them that what was keeping them from really excelling in customer service and results was that they were being distracted by all these little, itty-bitty jobs and customers. Since I was the Controller/IT person, I was the person they had to come to for a report of all the customers, ranked by annual sales. You can probably guess what we found: 80% of the sales came from 20% of the customers.

From that point forward, the whole focus of the company shifted. They were looking for a very specific customer and went about politely firing all the ones that didn't match. No one was running around doing extra work and handling emergencies for a $150 job. The employees could now give attention to customers who had weekly jobs of $10,000 or more.

What really happened was that, over the next few years, the focus got narrower and narrower. The number of clients didn't grow, but the revenue and profits rose exponentially. This little microfilm company in Carson, California, was generating a seven-figure, 25% net profit. The company was sold for an eight-figure amount, and my dad retired at age 55. It all began with that one report that I ran, and then management's execution of the plan: focusing on the vital few.

As Richard Koch wrote in *The 80/20 Principle*, "The 80/20 principle asserts that a minority of causes, inputs, or effort usually lead to a majority of the results, outputs, or rewards." Twenty percent of my dad's customers were generating 80% of the revenue and profit.

Lead vs. Lag Indicators

In the book *The 4 Disciplines of Execution*, by Chris McChesney, Sean Covey, and Jim Huling, they outline the concepts of *leading* indicators and *lagging* indicators. Sales and income are lagging indicators. We only see them *after* they have happened. When we are reflecting on sales for the past three months, we are looking in the past. In the moment that we are looking, we can have no impact on the result. It's already happened!

Leading indicators are the activities (usually only one, but maybe two) that lead to the results that we want to have. In real estate, the leading indicator is typically the number of people you spoke to in person or over the phone (that's what we mean by "making contact"). We can then create a "contact-to-sale ratio," meaning, the number of contacts it takes to make a sale. Achieving our sales goals becomes very simple: talk to more people and get better at talking to them. Beyond basic knowledge and competency, nothing else matters. A low contact-to-sale ratio is good! If your contact to sale ratio is 50:1, then talking to 50 people a week equates to 50 sales per year.

Here's the catch: When we are new in the business, our contact to sale ratio is more like 500:1, 10 times more than the seasoned agent at 50:1. So, we get in the business, and someone tells us to talk to people, do open house, etc. We do what they say, doing open house two weekends a month, making some phone calls, going to some networking events, etc. Four months later, we still have no sales. What the heck? What's happening? Well, assuming that we made 50 contacts per week—and that is a very generous number for many agents—it's been 16 weeks for a total of about 800 contacts. However, it isn't a precise cause and effect result. Just because we made 800 contacts doesn't guarantee "a sale" on the 500th person. It is an *average*. It is not uncommon to make 1,000 or more contacts before we make a sale and the numbers start working in our favor.

Most people quit. They give up way too early. They say that it isn't working. They look for other ways to generate business. They aren't clear on the leading indicator. *And they aren't tracking that number.*

In *The 4 Disciplines of Execution*, the disciplines were, essentially, (1) Focus on what's most important (they use the term *wildly*); (2) Take action on the leading measures; (3) Keep track (they use the term *scoreboard*; and (4) Create accountability.

Only in hindsight did I realize how fortunate I was to be in Steve's coaching program. These four disciplines had been part of his coaching program long before I met him in 2005—when you stop and think about it, they are common sense. What's most important: contacts. Action: for me, it became the doors. Scoreboard: Steve had an online scoreboard for everyone to login and track their numbers. Accountability: one of his best skills as a coach, we had weekly, then daily calls. By the way, what do people generally resist most? Accountability.

The 4 Disciplines of Execution was published in 2012, and Steve had been coaching agents for well over a dozen years by that point. It seems highly unlikely that he was wrong in his approach, given that this book became a bestselling book and a key component for companies' goal planning and implementation. You don't have to take my word for it, or Steve's—take the wisdom outlined in *The 4 Disciplines of Execution.*

Talking to People

How does this apply to real estate? Many real estate agents think that all activities matter the same. The key ingredient in a successful real estate practice (like almost every business) is sales. Not the sale of homes, but rather the acquisition of *clients* who are buying and selling homes. If you looked, for most successful agents, there is **one** thing that drives their business, and that is: *talking to people.*

What is the one thing that most agents **don't** do every day? Talk to people.

Talking to people every day is important, but not urgent (more on this in a moment).

NOTE: There are plenty of agents who built their business by *not* talking to people, but they did figure out what was most important. Maybe it was marketing, maybe they paid for leads, maybe they blogged or wrote articles. There *are* other ways to build a real estate business. Rest assured though that the 80/20 principle was in effect, and it was not immediate or easy.

Agents focus on what's in front of them, not unlike a dog. When I lived in California, we had two dogs, Brandy and Remy. They both loved to play fetch. They also liked to eat. I remember being in the yard, playing fetch with them, and one of the kids came outside with food in their hands. Remy stopped in mid-stride, reversed direction, and went for the kid with food. This is most real estate agents. They know that they need to talk to people, but they get distracted by the immediate gratification in front of them:

- A "maybe" customer calls to see a house.
- A client calls with a plumbing issue.
- A family member needs a ride somewhere.
- A vendor calls you and wants to take you to lunch.
- You can take a free class with free food, on how to spend more money on marketing and do no work and get 10 times more clients.

We let these distractions take us off course because we aren't clear on what is most important.

For 80% of us, the easiest, clearest, and most guaranteed way to succeed in real estate is to talk to people. Our job then becomes shockingly simple: figure out how to talk to people every day.

I too did not want to talk to people. Remember, I am an anti-social introvert. The last thing that I wanted to do was make phone calls. Parties? Not for me. Expireds and FSBOs? Forget it. I was desperate. I had to do something, and it finally became clear to me that the only way to make money was talking to people. The exception, of course, was that black hole called marketing. It seemed like spending lots of money could generate leads. But that seemed like the exception, it was not guaranteed, and that would be an expensive bet. That wasn't a gamble I could make.

For me, it came down to, "I must talk to people. And I am only going to knock on doors." That was my one thing. Do that thing every day, and it will all work out. There was going to be no more:

- Worrying.
- Busy work.
- Sitting in the office.

Essentially, I took the 80/20 rule and applied it even more granularly. Let's say that there are five ways you can talk to people: Door knock, phone calls to people that you know, phone calls to people you don't know, open house, and social networking (like going to parties and lunches). I picked one: knocking on doors. I did the 20% that would yield the 80%. Over the years, that has shifted a little. Over time, the number of people I knew and had in my database did grow, so I do have to make phone calls to people. In the beginning, it was through door knocking—80% of my business came from the doors, 20% came from other sources. Again, it all happened over time. It was the constant activity day in and day out that ultimately provided some results.

What's Urgent Is Whispering in Your Ear

It is hard to do the most important thing. It is easy to focus on what is in front of us.

It is hard to go out and knock on doors when we know several people have called us and are waiting on a call back. It is hard to explain to our family that we are not available all day, every day to attend to their needs. It can be hard for us to get that we *must* take care of certain things in order to fulfill our duties (to ourselves and our family).

It is easy to go to lunch. It is easy to wake up late. It is easy to get distracted. It is easy to get lulled by instant gratification.

It is hard to do what is most important; it is easy to do what's urgent. It is hard to do what is most important; it is easy to do what's urgent. I had many, many failed attempts at trying to do what's most important.

Over the years, it occurred to me that, if we succumb to the urgent and give in to instant gratification, we can expect the following impacts:

1. The whim of this moment is the thief of our future.
2. Sacrifice of our long-term fulfillment.
3. Sealing our fate of failure.
4. Guaranteeing that we will never really get what we want.
5. Giving up any and all control of our day and our life (because we are always "on call").
6. We don't have to do what is important . . . we can just live a life that is out of our control, like a bottle bobbing on the ocean.
7. We are saying that we are not important, devaluing who we are and what we do.

You could say that much of this list is similar and saying the same thing in several different ways—yup. Depending on how you come at it, the moment we give in to the moment, the thing that takes us off track, we are sacrificing our future goal. I can say with 100% certainty that every time, and I mean *every* time I have sacrificed—bailed on—my door-knocking appointment to handle an urgent client need, it was a complete waste of time. The biggest offender: the "now" buyer who has to see a property only in the window of my door knocking time. Whether it was an out-of-town prospect, or some new listing that came up that the buyer had to see in that timeframe, every single one of them was a waste of time. Every single one. None of them had to be done at that moment, and most of them did not turn into any future business. So, instead of doing the thing that generated business, I wasted that time. That was time that I never got back.

It really takes something to do only what's important. The allure of what is calling our attention is mesmerizing. It begs us to pay attention and not do what we are supposed to do.

One day, in spring of 2006, I was getting out of my car to knock on doors. Right as I was getting out of the car, Kathee, my escrow officer, called with an urgent matter: funding for my buyer's loan was short, and the property would not close that day. Now, my client, Jim, was a senior executive with Countrywide, the largest national mortgage originator at the time. His loan was being processed via their internal funding department, despite his reluctance to use them because of their reputation of incompetence, which is exactly what surfaced at the worst possible time.

Kathee had told me that she had already spoken to Jim and that he was handling it. Really, there was nothing for me to do. I couldn't do anything about the loan. I could have gone back to the office and "worried" about what was going to happen. I could have sat around waiting for things to get resolved and made myself "available." Instead, I hung up, shut my phone off, and went to the doors.

Two-plus hours later, I got back to my car, and turned on my phone. I called Kathee for an update. She proceeded to tell me that the file had closed even though the funds were short. Huh? How is that possible? Countrywide had funded the loan approximately $17,000 short of what was required, yet the transaction closed. I asked Kathee—she also had never seen this before—and she said that somehow Countrywide had guaranteed the funds to allow the deed to transfer.

Absolutely confused, I called my client. When we finally connected, he relayed how furious he had been. Not at me, but at the ineptitude of the Countrywide internal department. But the deal had closed, and still very intrigued, I asked what happened.

He laughed a little, and said, "I called the CEO, and when he got on the phone I said, 'Hey, it's Jim. CLOSE. MY. F#&@ING. LOAN . . . RIGHT. F#&@ ING. NOW.'" Then, he hung up. On the CEO! Miraculously, the loan was funded.

Now I have never had anything else even close to that happen again in my real estate career (fortunately). The real message, of course, is that the problem solved itself! In most cases, this is what will happen. Many problems and "urgencies" don't need us! *We need them*—to keep us from doing what we are supposed to do.

Don't give in. Just say no.

Then, go do what you are supposed to do.

Obstacles Never Stop Coming

I never wanted to knock on doors. Never. What I did was develop the habit of doing it. In 1940, Albert Gray famously delivered a speech entitled "The Common Denominator of Success." In it he said, "The common denominator of success—the secret of success of every man who has ever been successful—lies in the fact that he formed the habit of doing things that failures don't like to do." I was always afraid to get out of the car. Always. Still am. I *never* feel like doing it. Never. I just made knocking on doors a habit and did it anyway.

> *"The common denominator of success—the secret of success of every man who has ever been successful—lies in the fact that he formed the habit of doing things that failures don't like to do."*
> — *Albert Gray*

Over the years, of course, I got better, developed more skill, did more business and built more confidence. Although later in my career I had gotten to know thousands of people, many doors were (are) still "cold." I never know who is going to open the door, nor what will happen.

In February of 2017, I was about to knock on my 100,000th door. Yes, you read that right: 100,000th door. I finally felt like I was beginning to get some momentum. It felt like I had achieved something. Seriously, 100,000 doors—that's insane. Feeling extra invigorated, I go out this day to knock on doors. I get to 99,932. I know that the next day I will get to my 100,000th door. I am feeling really good.

That night, I get a two-minute voicemail from someone whose door I had knocked on that day. He called to complain. He said that he didn't like the postcard that I had left on his front porch, and he didn't like the idea of someone going door-to-door. Mind you, he wasn't home when I came by. I did not meet him. I knocked on his door and left a postcard underneath the mat. However, the real kicker came at the end of the voice mail: ". . . *and I spoke to every-one on the block, and they don't want you knocking on their door either.*"

Ouch. Knife through my heart, and then twisted really hard to make sure I was dead, and then, for good measure, kicked me on the ground after I stopped moving.

It cut right to my soul. (At that time) I had spent the previous 12 years—my entire real estate career—doing one thing and one thing only: knocking on doors. In that moment, it felt as if he had invalidated my entire existence as a real estate agent.

I thought about it for a while. Then it dawned on me: Hey, he just moved in. He doesn't know everyone on the block. *Many* people ***LOVE*** when I come by. I will show him! Sc*#w that guy!

And that is how the selfies started.

I knew that there were hundreds of people I had developed close relationships with. I also knew that sometimes, my coming to knock on a person's door actually made a difference–that I made a contribution to another human being. (I will talk more about this in chapter eight.) This ~~jerk~~ nice man had caused me to pause and consider what impact all this door knocking was having, and what I realized is that sure, there were plenty of people who had no interest in what I was doing. So what? It was all the other people who were thrilled (not kidding) that I came by. There were dozens more that were not clients (yet), but that had become great friends and referral partners.

About this same time, someone had told me about this app for your phone called Postagram. When you take a picture on your phone, you pull it up in this app, add a note, put in a name and address, and then they print and mail the postcard.

I put the two together: I started taking selfies with the people I loved, and then sent them the postcards. One of the first people I took a selfie with was Mr. Carlson. Approaching 90 years old, a little slower and a little more hunched over than he used to be— when I see Mr. Carlson, I just want to give him a big hug. Kind of like Winnie The Pooh, although his demeanor is more like Eeyore. He is funny, sweet, and genuine. When we were done chatting, I said, "Hey Mr. Carlson, let's take a picture."

He said, "A picture of me? Oh no." (Picture him saying it in an Eeyore voice.)

"No, a picture of both of us!"

"Both of us?" he asked.

"Yes, come on, it will be great!"

"All right," he said. We took the picture, I uploaded it into Postagram, and off it went. A few months later, I was back at Mr. Carlson's door again. He came to the door, greeted me, then leaned in and said, "That picture of us was pretty good, wasn't it?" With a big grin on his face! Amazing!

Doing what's most important is always what's most important.

5

THE END OF BEING OVERWHELMED

There Is Too Much to Do!

E ven when we are clear about what is most important, we don't often *do* what's most important. For one, almost nobody ever feels like doing lead generation (or anything else that is "hard"). Secondly, we have so much that we *could* be doing. We are now going to deal with reality—meaning, we are going to look at what's required in *doing* what's most important. "Doing" doesn't happen in a virtual reality, it happens in a physical reality. For instance, at this moment you're reading these words. You could be doing other things, but you are doing this. Same thing with your lead generation or going on a listing appointment. Those happen at specific times and places, that is what I mean by physical reality. In this chapter, we are going to lay out how you can start doing what's most important with freedom and flexibility.

One of my early mentors, Fred Wilson, said "*You can't do everything. When would you do it?*" I thought, "Yeah, when *would* I do everything?"

But most of us in real estate don't see it that way. We operate like there is a lot that we have to do *and* that we have to get it all done. We are busy reacting to what comes at us, like: chasing prospects who aren't going to do business with us, feeling busy with paperwork, responding to vendors' requests to go to coffee or lunch, signing up for and attending classes that we think we need but probably don't, office meetings, caravan or other property previewing, and getting our technology setup. We face a myriad of potential problems like: our car breaks, we lose our cell phone, or some emergency at home crops up and distracts us. Then, there are contract changes, economic cycles, political cycles, and everything else that affects the real estate market, like natural disasters. On top of all that, our clients have problems and issues that they expect us to solve. Finally, you can add in all the other stuff that you have to deal with that I didn't already mention.

As we already talked about, making contact is all we have to do . . . at least at first.

Seems simple enough. Why are we feeling like it's not that simple?

Because we don't believe it's that simple. We don't operate like it's that simple. We don't operate that way because not only do we not believe it, we aren't "set up" to operate that way. In other words, we don't have structures in place to manage our activity.

It is probably not unfair to say that selling real estate has become more complicated over time, and certainly transactions now have more moving parts. Contracts are longer and more intricate, financing is more rigorous, property inspections are more comprehensive, preparing a home for sale is more involved. In managing a real estate transaction, there are many little details that must get handled. That doesn't even include managing our own internal systems, like our client database, our financials, email management, cleaning out our voicemails, and capturing all the calls and text requests that we receive weekly. There are then projects that we have in regards to marketing—our website, social media, advertising, or other promotional work that we do. That is why it *feels* like there is so much happening, *and* we haven't even touched upon what's happening at home (kids, parents, friends, finances, house stuff, etc.).

We have an impossible belief that we must get everything done.

So, we have this dichotomy—on one hand, all we know is that there is the one thing we "should" do (make contact and do business), but on the other hand, we have *all these other things* coming at us. I am going to sum up our situation as follows:

1. We have an impossible belief that we must get everything done.
2. We have unreliable and/or ineffective systems and structures for handling all the inputs coming at us.

No wonder we feel overwhelmed and tell ourselves, *"There is just too much to do."*

Dealing with "Right Now"

As I said at the beginning of the chapter, "We can't do everything, when would we do it?" We can't do everything, we don't need to do everything, and everything will *not* get done—ever! We will always have things, lots of things, that don't get done and won't ever get done.

Pause. Please reread the previous paragraph.

All we can do is what we are doing right now, in this moment. Our entire day, in fact our entire life, is made up of "right nows." We can't make a phone call yesterday, nor can we go on an appointment tomorrow. We *can* make a phone call . . . right now. We can schedule an activity in the future, such as having lunch with a client next Friday at noon, by putting it as an occasion on our calendar. When next Friday at noon comes, there is still only the moment of "right now." In that moment in time, the only thing that we can and should be doing is having lunch with that client.

All we can do is what we are doing right now, in this moment.

Again, the point we must come to terms with (read this out loud to yourself): "I will never get it all done. Never ever."

Our job in life is not to "get it all done." Instead, consider that we have the things that are most important, and by doing those things, as Gary Keller says, "Make everything else easier or unnecessary."

If you have been in real estate for more than a month, you have long since realized that what is most important is generating business. Servicing the business comes second. If we don't have business to service, then we are out of business.

We can make overwhelm disappear.

When things are busy, the words that often come out of real estate agents' mouths are "I am so overwhelmed!" There is no such thing as "overwhelmed." It is made up. Go ahead, *show me* overwhelm. It doesn't exist. It is a story that we use to describe how we feel. We feel "overwhelmed" because there is more happening than we have the ability to process. Meaning, there are inputs and data points that are coming at us and we are not capturing them. We are not distinguishing what we will pay attention to and what we will ignore. We are not capturing and tracking things that are coming at us. We don't distinguish and give ourselves *permission* to ignore things that we will not handle right now. Finally, we aren't going to get everything done, but we are pretending that we will—and somehow, just maybe, we will magically have some extra time to get that "stuff" done. All of that creates an unease; we feel out of control or live inside this unmanageable context that we call "overwhelmed."

> *We are not distinguishing what we will pay attention to and what we will ignore.*

The path to disappearing overwhelm is distinguishing what *it* is and how it got there. We need to get that we are the ones going around saying, "I'm overwhelmed" or "I have too much to do." *We* create that statement out of *our* mouths! It is fine to say that things are "active." It is fine to acknowledge that there are many things happening. What there is to get is that we must be aware and responsible about how we contextualize what's happening.

After we acknowledge the language that we are using to describe what our circumstances are, *then* we can deal with physical structures. We must have a system for dealing with all the inputs, activities, and commitments in our lives. How are we capturing new information? How are we determining what we work on? When are we working on this? When are we working on that? The work must get planned—and scheduled.

What's missing: introducing capture tools and operating from a calendar/schedule.

Just because we have a smartphone and other technology at our fingertips does not mean that we have the appropriate tools and systems. Many agents (and human beings) don't have the appropriate systems to capture all the information with which we are dealing. However, when we do have systems to capture inputs, our brain is not busy and preoccupied trying to remem-

We have unreliable and/or ineffective systems and structures for handling all the inputs coming at us.

ber things. Our brain is not designed to be a capture tool. The moment that we capture all the information around us, we are freeing up space so that we can now be present and focus on the task at hand. We don't have to be thinking about all the other things that we could do, should do, need to do later. We are only focused on this moment. The access to this freedom is to have a system, or methodology, for processing and handling all that there is "to do."

I recommend two methodologies that have helped me the most. The first is David Allen's Getting Things Done approach (GTD). GTD, which has been around since the late '90s and has been widely adopted across the world, predominantly in the corporate world (but certainly not exclusively). Allen's main point is to have a mind like water—empty, still. Our head is the *worst* place to capture and remember things.

The second methodology is Mission Control (www.MissionControl.com). Mission Control is a proprietary methodology implemented by licensed trainers (so, no public forums, no book that you can buy). It works to reframe the view that we have of our work and what there is to do. Although there are tools and structures to implement, its overall effectiveness has to do with seeing our work from a totally different perspective. In implementing Mission Control, "we have too much to do" will be removed from our vocabulary.

For right now, the thing to get is that, regardless of what methodology you use, you *must* have one! Without reliable systems and structures to handle the many moving parts of our business and our lives we will be unable to be present and effective.

What is meant by the term "being present"? It means being available in the moment. Not wondering what to do next, not wondering if we remembered to do something, not wondering what to say next, not wondering or thinking about what we are making for dinner. Being present means that we are right there in the moment, listening and paying attention to what is in front of us. It is a skill. It is something that we learn to do. It starts with getting everything out of our head, and having systems and processes for storing and retrieving information and tasks. Like GTD, the key is to empty our mind of all the stuff that can be captured and stored somewhere else.

In this moment, we can only do what we are doing "right now." We can't do what we're not doing right now—we can't do what we are doing later, or yesterday. There is only right now. There is way more to do than we will ever get to. We will never get it all done. Never. Acknowledging and living from this point of view is a paradigm shift. It takes much practice.

If we can be "okay" with never getting it all done, then we are left with choices about what we *are* going to do and what we are not. We are left with what we are doing now, what we are "not doing now," and what we are "never doing now." What we are doing now is what we have scheduled on our calendar. Everything else goes on two lists of stuff that we might someday schedule to be worked on.

Both of these methodologies are amazing. You can do one, both, or something else that works for you. The key is to have a framework to operate from. In both of these methodologies, there is one thing that is absolutely consistent: We must operate from a schedule, and we do that by using a calendar. Our calendar is what drives our existence. It essentially becomes our to-do list. If we have never fully operated from these methodologies—it is going to take some practice. Be prepared for it to take some time. It might be many months before you really get in the rhythm of it, that's okay!

Is It Really Possible to Schedule in the Chaos of Real Estate?

You're probably thinking that it is absolutely impossible to plan your days; in real estate there are simply too many different things that can come up and require our attention.

Back to Stephen Pressfield and *The War Of Art:* He relates the following story regarding schedule. Somerset Maugham, who was once asked if he writes on a schedule or by inspiration, replied (paraphrased), "I write by inspiration. Fortunately, it strikes me every morning at 9 a.m. sharp."

> *"A schedule defends from chaos and whim."*
> — *Annie Dillard*

In 2019, John Maxwell received the Master of Influence Award by the National Speakers Association. He gave a brief acceptance speech, and then he was interviewed on stage by Nido Qubein. John Maxwell, whose books have sold millions of copies, regularly speaks to Fortune 500 companies and has internationally been recognized as one of the preeminent experts on leadership. It would not be unfair to say that he has accomplished quite a bit, more than most, and really does not *need* to do anything else. Yet every morning he writes. When he is home, he writes from 6:30 to 11:30 a.m. Every morning. If he is on the road, then it might be only an hour. Either way, it gets done. Now, does John Maxwell really need to write every day? Doesn't he have enough books? Hasn't he made enough impact? If John Maxwell can make the time to do what is most important every day (for him, writing; for us, making our contacts), would it be crazy to think that the same thing applies to us?

After we have scheduled our "writing" (i.e., our lead generation), then what? How do we schedule and plan for what seems like the randomness and chaos of real estate? Consider that many of us don't do certain tasks every day nor necessarily every week. For example, the actual selling of homes. For many of us, we can sell $10MM, $20MM, or more by selling only 15–25 houses per year. That means we don't have listing or showing appointments every day. We are not writing contracts, negotiating contracts, or going on appointments every day. However, just because we don't do those things every day doesn't mean that we shouldn't plan for them. For me, it worked out that I should plan to have all my appointments at one time: weekdays from 2 to 5 p.m. Now, have I ever done an appointment outside those times? Of course. However, I plan for that time, and that is where I work to push all my appointments. Know what? That is where 80% of my appointments happen! (Remember the 80/20 rule?)

Plan for the rule, not the exceptions. We *feel* like we need to plan for the exceptions; however, when you stop and think about it, does it make sense to do it that way? Is it unfair to say that most of what "comes up" is stuff that we know will come up, we just don't know exactly when it will happen? If we plan in advance for how we will handle those things, it becomes much easier to schedule. Even John Maxwell, when he is on the road and not following his "usual" schedule, can adjust and still accomplish his most important work.

There Are Just Too Many Things I Could Be Doing

Okay, so we know that we need to operate from a schedule. We get that, but we don't do it. Why . . . why in the world do we know that we need to operate from a schedule but don't?

One reason may be that we have too many options of what we *could* be doing. Deciding what we will do becomes exhausting. Consider: We have too much choice and freedom. In the book, *The Paradox of Choice*, Barry Schwartz says that having no choice is as insufferable as being in a concentration camp. Having more choice does liberate and fuel us, while increasing the quality of our lives—until it doesn't. At some point, too much choice leads to debilitation.

Schwartz describes an example of a study done in a store where they gave away free samples of jam. When people were presented with six jams to sample from, 30% of them bought a jar after sampling. However, when they gave people more choice—more jars to choose from—the ability to decide and purchase went down. In the second example, customers were exposed to 24 different jams to sample from, resulting in only 3% of them making a purchase. A large array of options discourages action/decision, because it causes too much effort to make a decision. Consumers—that would be us—decide not to decide.

It hurts our head when we have so many things that we could be doing. Trying to figure out what we could do, should do, or feel like doing—it's too hard. It's exhausting. Like the customers exposed to the 24 jars of jam—we don't buy, but in our case, *we do nothing—we don't take action*. That is why having "white space" on our calendar is *not* helpful. In fact, it fosters indecision and fatigue. There is too much choice!

That is why we must start with what is most important. Once we get that done, in some respects, it doesn't matter what else happens or comes at us for the rest of the day. We have so much that we *could* be doing, and so many things that *could* come at us. Waiting and planning for that is paralyzing. As the saying goes, "Doing the most important thing is always the most important thing." So, let's have that most important thing identified and scheduled *first*.

There's Lots of Blank Space in My Calendar

We must work from a calendar. Full disclosure: I have spent many years struggling with this item. Yet, we must work from activities that are *scheduled*. Starting with the *most important* activity, ideally earlier in the day than later. Why?

As Gary Keller outlined in *The ONE Thing*, willpower is not on call, and there is not an infinite supply of willpower. It is like a battery charge. Every day, we wake up with a full charge of willpower. It is drained by use as we go through the day, until eventually we are as malleable as silly putty. For me it often looks like this: I get home, and someone in the house has the television on, tuned to a show that I don't watch or care for, but next thing I know, I stand there for 20 minutes watching. My ability to decide, and act, has evaporated. I am sucked into whatever was put in front of me.

Time-blocking means making appointments on a calendar, and then . . . wait for it . . . actually doing what is on our calendar.

Doing what is most important should be done as soon as possible. That's why John Maxwell writes first thing in the morning. That's why Somerset Maugham wrote at 9 a.m. sharp. It's why almost every sales trainer or coach tells us to do our prospecting first thing in the day.

This is the one area where I had consistent success over the years. I don't mean that I was perfect at it. I mean that I actually did the work the majority of the time. I had *way* more wins than losses. I scheduled my door knocking, which was most important, and I did it. Thousands of times.

Time-blocking means making appointments on a calendar, and then . . . wait for it . . . actually doing what is on our calendar. This is very simple. Yet mostly this does not happen. Well, some appointments happen. A doctor's appointment. Maybe a spin class or workout scheduled with a trainer or an accountability partner. An appointment with a client. A haircut.

What appointments often don't get scheduled? Or if they are scheduled, they get "missed?" An appointment to prepare our monthly financial statement. An appointment to pay bills or review anything financial (yes, a small percentage of people love this stuff and can't wait to do it—most agents though don't). An appointment to make phone calls. An appointment to do lead generation.

Scheduling an appointment on a calendar gives something reality in space and time. If we say to our best friend, "Hey, let's get together and have coffee," and our friend replies, "Yes, we should do that," what happens? Nothing! Is our coffee get-to-gether going to happen? Probably not. It has no date, time, or place. *When* are we going to meet for coffee? Saturday? Three months from now? What *time? Where?*

The same thing happens when we say, "I need to talk to everyone in my database four times a year." *When* are we going to make those calls? For me, I have made these calls on the days when the weather was not good for the doors. I knew that every month there would be several days where the doors are not an option, or not ideal. Those days, I made calls instead of going to the doors. Either way, it went down as an occasion in my calendar.

Why We Don't Want to Work from a Calendar

We don't like being tied to something so rigid. Remember, most of us got into real estate for freedom and flexibility!

I have never wanted to work from a calendar. Most of my career, I have failed at it. I try and try and try.

The things that we "feel" like doing—going on a listing appointment—are easy to put on a calendar. We aren't talking about those things. Most agents have no problem putting those appointments on a calendar and keeping them.

I am talking about using our calendar as our "teacher." When we were in school, we followed a schedule. We knew what period was next, we went to each class at the scheduled time, and, in each class, the teacher had a plan for what was happening during that period. We may not have liked every period, we may not have liked every teacher, and we may have really disliked some of what we did in each class—but we knew what we were supposed to do every day. We did not think about where we were going and what we were doing. It was already decided for us.

Most people resist being told what to do. To be human, especially in free, first-world countries, is to have free will. Many people do not equate free will with following a schedule. Free will means being free!

Consider that we have it backward. Consider the "free will" part is wrapped up in the school schedule. When it has already been decided ahead of time what we are going to do, our mind is freed up to focus on the task at hand. We take away the energy and angst caught up in, "What should I do next?"

> *"There is no more miserable human being than one in whom nothing is habitual but indecision . . ."*
> — *William James*

The hardest part about being a real estate agent: there is no school schedule. There is no one telling us and making us follow a productive schedule. Instead, we are on our own. No boss. No teacher. No one to scold us if we are tardy.

The people who have the easiest time succeeding in real estate are those that create the structure of a schedule immediately in their business. They begin with setting start and end times to the day—just like school. They schedule certain activities during the day, like "their classes." They could schedule their "hardest" classes earlier in the day to get them over with. Then, of course, we have "lunch" or "recess." For some people that actually means taking time away for lunch to relax, or maybe taking clients out for lunch. Recess might mean a midday workout or yoga class. For me, having a break in the middle of the day is important. Knocking on doors is physically and mentally challenging. Frankly, being an introvert—I am wiped out. I need quiet time. What I really need is a nap. Many days, I take one right in my car. Now, that might not be your thing. No problem—do your thing and do not feel guilty about it!

My point is that, if you do what is most important first, the rest of the day flows much easier. And many days, there is time for a nap.

6

CREATING CERTAINTY AMIDST THE CHAOS

Real Estate Is Uncertain

We have no control over when buyers buy and when sellers sell.

We can't make a buyer come see a house and buy it. We don't control our client's circumstances. The inspectors, appraisers, lenders, title companies, attorneys and all the other participants' actions in a transaction are also out of our control. So, why do we think that we are at the center of it, that we should be available 24/7 to handle and fix any issue that comes up?

The truth is that we have no control over the circumstances of a real estate transaction. Consider that when we operate and make ourselves available 24/7 to handle problems, we are giving space for problems to show up. We're also never free to be present in other areas. We are tied to our phone (whether it's a call, text, or email), waiting for the next issue to arise. We sit around waiting for the day to grab us instead of the other way around.

I am not saying that an active real estate business doesn't have lots of unplanned issues that need to be handled. I *am* saying that we can plan to have surprises and be prepared for them while we still tend to what's most important. Going back to the example where my buyer's loan closed short—that was a big problem, and yet it did not need me, nor did it give me an excuse to not do what was most important that day (going to the doors).

We know what we need to do every day, we know why we are doing it, and we have it scheduled, but Resistance is pulling at us. It often shows up as a distraction. Emergencies or urgent matters fool us into thinking that it's okay to not do what we need to do.

This chapter is not talking about the nitty gritty details of how to use a calendar and other low-level tactics. This is high-level, this is your overall framework and approach, maybe even part of your guiding principles. We are talking about having a process and a routine.

Process and Routine Can Give You Comfort and Stability

Knocking on doors is my process and routine. The first 15 years of my real estate career were as simple as tying my shoes: I knocked on doors. That was it. I had nothing else to do. Don't get me wrong, there were (and are) many, many times when I wanted to do something else. I wanted to get distracted with marketing, or social media, or something more glamorous. Of course, there were days that I wanted to do *anything* that was more comfortable than knocking on doors.

Really, the comfort was in the *process and routine* of knocking on doors. For 150-plus days a year, the day looked very much the same. How I prepare for the doors, what time I drove to the doors, where I parked the car, how I got myself out of the car, how I took breaks, how I wrapped up, etc. It was all the same. Sure, it had been modified with efficiency over the years, but essentially it looks exactly the same as it did toward the beginning.

What I finally discovered: The routine of knocking on doors gave me predictability and consistency in my real estate business that, by its very nature, is unpredictable and uncertain. I found comfort and stability in controlling my actions day in, day out, and these actions are what mattered most to my long-term success.

> *The routine of knocking on doors gave me predictability and consistency in my real estate business that, by its very nature, is unpredictable and uncertain.*

This is a business where things are typically viewed as chaotic and unpredictable, starting with how we get paid. We do not get a paycheck! We only get paid if we close a sale, which is subject to many circumstances out of our control and influence.

As we said earlier, we can't control:

- When people are ready to buy and sell.
- The buyer or seller's circumstances: job loss, transfer, etc.
- Our clients' emotional states.
- The financing process, including appraisal and underwriting.
- Inspections and repairs.
- The closing itself: attorneys, title, escrow— other players with their own agendas and timelines.

Real estate seems easy from the outside, but we all know that it is quite hard. That is why we get paid a commission. The angst of not knowing when we will get paid, where our next client and transaction is coming from—it's very unsettling and very stressful (for most of us). Even longtime, high-producing agents have waves of *"Am I ever going to sell a house again?"* Almost all of us have dealt with this . . . repeatedly.

The routine is what saves us. The routine is what gives us comfort amongst the chaos. Ryan Holiday, author of many bestselling books, describes it in *Stillness Is the Key* as "routine becomes ritual," which is exactly what happened in my real estate business. The ritual of knocking on doors gives me space. Space for what? Space for dealing with everything else, including the gaps between waves of business. What I never worried about was what I was going to do every day. That part was handled because I knew what was most important. It was scheduled, and I did it.

Steve's coaching to me was spot on: focus on the process. That advice took away all the "mental gymnastics" about what to do every day. You know— should I go to the doors today? Should I make my sphere and open house calls? Should I preview houses and find people to talk to? Should I make phone calls to the neighbors around a new listing? Should I go through old lead lists? Maybe I should just invest in marketing and leverage myself?

I didn't have to worry about *any* of that stuff! Now, from time to time, did I get tempted with that type of thinking? Of course, I am human. As we talked about with scheduling, all I have to do is follow the schedule. The most important thing is scheduled, and that is what I am doing. That frees me up to be present in the moment. I don't have to be worried or concerned about anything else. Those things will get handled later, when they are scheduled. In the meantime, I can rest in the fact that I am doing the most important thing in my day. *That* is what gives me peace and comfort.

Habits

Every day we are operating from habits and routines, often without realizing it. We say that we are going to work out. We say that we are going to eat healthier. We say that we are going to be kinder to our significant other, or our parents, or our children. We say that we will meditate, or do yoga. We say that we will do those things today.

When the day is over, have all those things been done? Maybe we didn't wake up on time. We didn't exercise. We didn't plan out our meals for the day or week ahead of time. We didn't get to our most important activities. Therefore, what habits are we reinforcing? The habit of _not_ doing something. We don't feel good in those moments, we feel the opposite: We feel bad. We feel guilty. The feelings of disappointment and frustration can become our default. It is no accident that we feel that way. We broke our word—we broke our agreement to ourselves, which is the most important and difficult agreement we make. We often operate like it's no big deal, almost as if it doesn't exist, because often it's not explicitly declared. Consider that we are disempowered when we don't honor what comes out of our mouth. Whether we are aware of it or not, breaking our word to ourselves is working against us. The day before I edited this paragraph, I did something stupid on my scheduling and missed my door knocking slot. That doesn't happen often, but when it does I am completely disempowered; in fact, I get very moody. In this case, I was somewhat depressed for almost a whole day. I didn't keep my most important agreement, in the middle of writing a book on keeping my agreements! The best thing that I can do for my mental state and keeping my temperament high: keep my agreements, beginning with the ones I make to myself.

One other remarkable story about Somerset Maugham, the writer, comes from his response to the question, "Mr. Maugham, do you like to write?" His reply, "Well, no, I like the experience of _having writ-_

ten." When I first heard this, I immediately equated the scenario to exercising/going to the gym. Many of us don't like exercising, but we like the feeling of *having exercised.*

I have exercised almost my entire life—and I really don't enjoy doing it. Since the seventh grade, I cannot think of too many times where I went more than a few weeks or a month that I did not exercise. The reason that I exercised: I liked the *feeling of being healthy.* I like the way that my body feels and looks by being vital and alive. I like being able to ski, run, and play with my kids. Some of that is probably ego driven—I *am* from Los Angeles, the epicenter of "looking good"—but there is no denying the positive health and mindset benefits that exercising has given to me. It is one of the most important things in terms of my overall well-being.

When it comes to our business, the same thing applies. There is *the* most important activity that we *must* do every day to achieve our goals. If we can establish the habit of doing this, then we can create a process and make it routine.

I chose to knock on doors every day. Why? Well, for one, what else was I going to do? Second, it was very simple. No call lists to obtain. No social events to schedule. Everything was in my control: when I went, how long I went. I had one thing to do every day, and that was it. There was nothing else that I had to worry about. What I did not realize at the beginning: the real power was in building the habit of doing it. Getting to the doors year in and year out, 150-plus times per year, created the habit of knocking on doors. I was never perfect. Stuff did come up.

I took time off, I had client-related issues come up, training classes, events with my family. It did rain from time to time in Los Angeles. In Colorado, it gets cold sometimes, and sometimes—it snows!

Making the agreement to knock five days a week meant that I was planning to do that five days a week. Even if it snowed one day, or I had some other event, then I still had more opportunities to do the task than not. Conversely, where I saw people get tripped up: They plan on knocking (I am using this as an example, but you can apply it to some other most important activity) three days a week, like Monday-Wednesday-Friday. Then what happens? Monday comes, and a child is sick, so they miss on Monday. Wednesday comes, and the weather is bad. By the time Friday has come, they have already missed two out of two opportunities. They have created the habit of "not doing." The emotional resilience to "make it" on Friday is low. It is very easy to build the excuse, "Ah, this week is blown, I will start *next* week." We all know what happens the following week. The same cycle repeats. It is the habit of "not" doing.

I am not kidding—that really happens. What's worse is when people build a habit of doing over several months, and *then* lose their way. They worked hard to get in the groove, then they go on vacation, they miss a week or two for some other emergency or illness. Then, they "come back to work" and they are putting out fires or playing catch-up. Or they get busy doing business. Next thing they know it's one, two, or six months later. The habit that they did not put back in place is prospecting. The end result is that they fell back into the habit of not doing.

Creating an Environment and Structure that Supports the Habit

I never wanted to knock on doors. Never. I never ever felt like it. I would much rather have done a million other things.

So, if it's something that I never ever want to do, how have I done it all these years? First, I had a *why* and no Plan B. Then, I figured out what activity was most important. Then, I made that activity a habit. That might seem like an oversimplification. Having said that, there are a few things that I did learn and apply in habit forming that are worth mentioning.

The first thing I learned: Create an "environment" that supports the action I want to make a habit. James Clear states in his bestselling book, *Atomic Habits*, "Environment is the invisible hand that shapes human behavior." For me, it started with my car. Why not have everything that I need to door knock in my car? That included the shoes that I wear, the materials that I hand out, hats, sunscreen, and my name tag. There is a box in my car that never comes out. These are my tools, and the tools never leave the car. The exception: December, when I take time off from the doors, the box comes in, I go through everything, and clean it out and reorganize it for the upcoming year.

> *"Environment is the invisible hand that shapes human behavior."*
> —James Clear

Next: Create a system for knocking on doors. I figured out which neighborhoods I was going to knock. Then, I started at one end of the neighborhood and would keep going until I finished that neighborhood. I don't have to wonder where I am going every day. It is already decided—I start where I left off. Now, I sometimes get the question, "What neighborhood to start in?" It doesn't matter. Pick one. It can always be adjusted later. The key, of course, is to plan out and decide what's being done ahead of time—not in the morning before I head out the door.

The same goes for materials to be handed out. As I mentioned before, I wasted a lot of time futzing with postcards and handouts right before I went to the door. That was a terrible thing to do! It caused distractions, made me late, and often left me flustered and not present. What gets handed out is the *least* important piece of the process, but if you are going to leave something at the door, then the preparation of those materials is done ahead of time.

NOTE: If you are building your business on marketing, you would disagree with the statement about what gets left at the doors. Additionally, if you are going to door knock around an open house, it *is* a good idea to leave behind an invitation about the open house. However, these are ancillary notes and not the main point of not getting distracted from the main activity: talking to people.

Create a routine that works, then follow it:

- How I approach the door is always the same.

- How I take notes at the door is the same.
- How I follow up with people is always the same.

How I do everything is . . . the same! I am not changing it every month or every quarter. I finally learned to make the decision once, and then stick to it. I have freed up my mind to focus on being present with the people in front of me. I am freed up to deal with other issues or projects that require my time and effort. Deciding about what to hand out, how to follow up with people—total waste of time and energy. I know this because I've done it before and wasted a lot of time!

Okay, so knocking on doors isn't for everyone. You may never knock on a door, no problem. The same approach can be applied to other activities. Here are two examples:

- **Sphere calls:** Have a list, or set up your CRM, to give you the 10, 20, or more calls that you need to make that day. DO IT THE DAY BEFORE! Or the week before, or at the beginning of the year! If you have 500 people in your database, you could decide, "I make 10 calls per day out of my database." If it is done four days per week, that's 40/ week. It will take you about three months, or one quarter, to make those calls. How do you know whom to call? Start at *A* and go to the end, then repeat. Maybe you have vacation and holiday time mixed in. (I only plan my year to work 40 weeks.) With that simple exercise, you would contact everyone in your database three times per year via phone.

- **<u>Open house:</u>** If you want to build your business via open house, how many open houses are you going to do? Plan out those days at the beginning of the year, or at a minimum set them up for the quarter. Set up your system for doing open house so that it becomes routine.

Now, we have a system and we have a routine. How does it become ritual? For me, it came down to two things: (1) an environment that supports my schedule, and (2) honoring my agreement with myself about what I was going to do. Then, work like heck to keep those two things in place. *Eventually* it becomes ritual. The key word: *eventually*, meaning "over time." How long will it take for you? I don't know. I know that for me it was measured in years.

Having an environment support us is telling everyone else when we are available and when we are not. If a client, family member, or an associate asks us to do something in our blocked time—the answer to their request is "NO!" That may seem harsh; however, that is the *only* answer. I mean, you could say it a little nicer than that, but the answer is still the same.

When I was married and my kids were little, if my wife wanted me to take the kids to the doctor or do something with them, she knew to schedule it in the afternoon—*after* my door knocking. If a client or business partner wanted to meet for lunch: "No can do." I don't do lunch because it is in the middle of my door knocking time—unless they want to eat lunch at 2 p.m. For many people that didn't work, so we didn't do lunch. Here's the thing: People who were around me got to learn my schedule. They stopped tempting me with offers to be distracted because I literally trained them to support my habit and routine. Ann, my transaction manager for more than 10 years, knew not to schedule closings or inspections during my blocked time. I never had a problem because she was working to help keep my schedule.

The second piece to making our routine become ritual is centered around keeping promises to ourselves.

Keeping Our Promises

There is another force at work: It is the power of keeping a promise. We often discount the power of keeping this promise, mostly because it does not occur to us as a promise. It occurs, often, as something we "should" do, not something we must do. We often don't powerfully promise that we will do our most important thing at a specific time.

In my experience, promising something and fulfilling on that promise builds character. It creates momentum. It has integrity. When I say integrity, I do not mean morality. I mean workability. In other words, having form and function that works. For example, if we are building a house, does the foundation have integrity? Is it structurally sound? Does it have a form that will last? Will it hold firm in a wind or snow storm? Will it persist over time? The same applies to us. Does what we say—and do—have any integrity?

For example, if we tell a client we will be at their house at 3 p.m., and we show up at 3:05, what have we demonstrated? We have demonstrated being late. We said 3 p.m., but showed up at a different time. Now, you can go down the path of, "Well, it was only five minutes!" There are whole essays, seminars, and books on this topic—but for right now, consider that there is no gray. On the topic of keeping our word and being on time, or anything else that we give our word (promise) to, we either do what we say or we don't. Period. And I really mean *period.*

If we tell someone that we will follow up and we don't. If we tell someone that we will send them an email on something and then don't. If we tell some-one that we will meet them at 3:00 p.m. and we get there at 3:05. Those are all examples of us *not* keep-ing our promise. Again, it may have not occurred to us in the moment as promises, but consider that they are.

People who do what they say have an extra level of workability in their lives. They say something, then they do it. They aren't spending time worrying about things that they didn't do, they aren't always coming up with rationalizations and excuses why they didn't do what they said they would do. Think back to the example of showing up at 3:05 p.m. (which was late). What thought came into your mind? For some people, they were thinking, "Ah, it's only five minutes. That's not really a big deal." Or, they go to, "Well, there is probably a good reason." Often, we go to really good excuses, such as: My other meeting went long, I got stuck in traffic, I entered the wrong address in my GPS, etc. Who cares what the reason was? It makes no difference in the outcome. The reason does not make it okay that we didn't keep our promise.

So, why in the world am I spending all this time on "being on time" or this "other nonsense" about promising and keeping promises? Because there is power in keeping our promises—especially to ourselves. If we know what we need to do every day, and then we do it, that day is a success—regardless of any other outcome. We kept our word to ourselves, and that is a win!!! If we can do that day in, day out, then we are building the habit of fulfilling what we say. That creates a space of workability, responsibility, and attracts and creates opportunity (and sales)!

Back to Somerset Maugham: I do not like knocking on doors, but I do like the feeling of *having knocked*. My process and routine are how I maintain the regular experience of having knocked.

7

PATIENCE VS. INSTANT GRATIFICATION

We All Want It Now

Almost no one is willing to wait for anything, particularly when it comes to our own success. Resistance is waiting for and counting on our impatience. Resistance tells us, "This isn't working. Nothing is happening. You should be worried and concerned. You should switch tactics, or maybe . . . just give up!"

In a marathon or other endurance race, do we get the medal at the beginning? Of course not. That would be ridiculous. We have to toughen up, slog it out, and demonstrate that we have trained and prepared. We have to go do the work, *then* we get the medal. So, why in the world do we think that we should get the medal first in other areas of our life—especially in our real estate business?

For some reason, we have it in our heads that everyone else is an overnight success. Sure, if you turn on the television (if anyone still does that), or go onto your phone or computer, the Interwebs are full of pictures, videos, and stories of all these people who have "made it." From the scroll on our phones it sure looks like everyone else is "winning and succeeding."

> *"The prizes of life are at the end of each journey, not near the beginning."*
> — Og Mandino,
> *The Greatest Salesman in the World*

When we look more closely, however, consider that the concept and appearance of an overnight success is a deception. It's like a duck: People see the beautiful duck gracefully floating through the water—what they don't see is the frenzied activity beneath the surface. Where does the duck sleep at night? In a fancy duck house, or hidden in some bush, so that it doesn't get eaten overnight? How long does that duck actually live? What about the duck's chicks—did they all survive? Where are all the Instagram pictures of the duck living it up?

Oh wait, there aren't any, because ducks don't live that way! Neither do we—at least, not naturally. In our current modern world, it is all about comfort and "having things." Depending on what part of the country (or world) we live in, it is not hard to be deceived. Drive to a mall or shopping district, and we will likely find lots of beautiful people dressed in fancy clothes and driving fancy cars. It sure looks like all these people have "made it."

When you go to a real estate sales meeting or some other real estate agent gathering—what do we see? Much of the same thing. It looks like everyone is killing it. People talk about how great they are, how amazing things are, and it sure looks like everything is fabulous on the surface.

Now, for some people, the success we see may really be true. Their business is doing well, they are doing well, and they are experiencing waves of success. However, if you look behind the curtain, what is going on? Meaning:

- How long have they been in business?
- What effort and money got them to where their business is right now?
- What struggles did they endure (or are still enduring)?
- How long were they going at it with mediocre results?

I can think of five high-producing agents ($500,000 to $1MM-plus in GCI) that I know personally, and I can say for certain that their first five to 10 to 15 years in the business did not look *anything* like their current state.

Mostly, when we look at the facts, people have endured a difficult and prolonged journey to get where they are now. The phrase that seems to capture the essence of this phenomenon: "It only took 10 years to become an overnight success." If you are familiar with Anders Ericcson's work on the 10,000-

hour rule—success takes time. It takes time to be good at anything. Sure, there are hacks to shorten the time. As author/podcaster/entrepreneur Tim Ferriss likes to point out, there are shortcuts to get decent competency. For example, when learning a foreign language, Ferriss learned the 300 most frequently used words to get up and running quickly. But we aren't talking about decent competency, we are talking about longevity and mastery.

There are plenty of people who have a good first year, or a good year in general, because they hustled their butt off. Maybe they got a little lucky. We are not talking about them. We are also not talking about the person who is "the one"—the one person who is rookie of the year. The one person who is killing it from day one. Most of us are not *that* person. If that person is you, congratulations, but likely the person who is the one in a 100 is not reading this book. So, for the rest of us . . .

Our Addiction to Instant Gratification

We are addicted to instant gratification. At the time of this writing, technology allows us to be heading home from work in a car that is not ours because we pushed a button on our phone and a car came and picked us up. While in the car, we can push some other buttons on our phone and have sushi delivered to our house. If we would like a vodka martini to go with our sushi, we can order that too. As we pull up to our home, so do two other cars, with our sushi and libation.

If we want to know any piece of trivia, no problem: The phone that is always at our side can give us the answer. What's the weather tomorrow? What's the score of the game? Where is my friend's flight (i.e., she is on her way to Africa, let me look up where it is and how it's going). Infinite possibilities to get information abound that were inconceivable when this century began. Now it's common practice, and we are addicted to it. Especially if you were born after 2000—there is no knowledge or memory of when information was not instantaneous.

I was watching the movie *Pretty Woman* with my teen daughter. That movie came out in 1990 (my daughter was born in 2005). It was a popular and successful movie, becoming part of the pop culture, complete with movie references and even fashion (remember the brown, polka-dot dress that Julia Roberts wears to the polo match?). Watching the movie 30 years later, my daughter does not know any of this. She had sort of heard of Julia Roberts, but not really.

If you saw the movie, you may remember that there is the house limousine of the Regent Beverly Wilshire Hotel that drives Richard Gere everywhere. Toward the end, Julia Roberts is being driven home from her week at the hotel. In this scene she is alone in the car, and through the rear window is the boomerang-looking antenna, affixed to the trunk of the car. I paused the movie and asked my daughter if she knew what that was—which, of course, she did not. I said that was the television antenna. "Huh?" she replied. I explained that it was a big deal to have a television in the limo, but you needed an antenna to get reception for the main channels.

This was completely foreign to her. She has never watched "regular" television. We were watching *Pretty Woman* "on demand"—when we decided to watch the movie, we put on the smart television, paid for the rental, and began watching. Instantly.

It. Is. Everywhere. We are addicted to it, and Resistance is thrilled.

Nothing Is Happening

If we are impatient creatures addicted to instant gratification at least some of the time, what happens when we are not getting immediate results? We say, "Nothing is happening"; "I am not getting any results"; or "I am doing all this stuff, but I have nothing to show for it."

Good. Resistance wants us to think that. Resistance wants us to get frustrated and quit. For probably 80% of us realtors, that is exactly what happens. The 80% who quit look for the easy way out. They look for the instant gratification. They don't see anything happening on the surface, so they either keep switching tactics or quit altogether.

What gets missed is that we progress over time, and in the moment it can look like nothing is happening. In real estate, remember that our sales are a *lagging* indicator. We have no control over when a sale happens. For most of us, the key metric to our leading indicator is the number of people we talk to. In the markets where I have sold and done the most coaching and training, it takes, on average, 250–500 contacts to make a sale—if you are a newer or less-experienced agent. It hovers between 100–250 for an agent that has a few years in the business but hasn't quite broken through yet. The real progress/success/mastery comes into play when the contact-to-sale ratio drops below 100.

This progression takes time! It also takes much effort and lots of failure. We just think that we should automatically be at the low contact-to-sale ratio. However, most of us don't track our numbers, so we don't even know how many contacts we are making. We may start knocking on doors, doing open houses, or calling our sphere. After a few weeks we begin to get impatient. After three months, many of us have quit—because, like my former dog Remy, we get distracted and taken off course. For those of us that stuck around for three months, we say, "Hey, where are all my sales? I was doing all this work, and nothing happened!"

Well, let's look. After 12 weeks, assuming that we made 50 contacts per week—that's 600 contacts. That may be good for . . . perhaps . . . *one* sale. Of course, this is not an exact cause and effect—it's not like on the 500th contact a sale magically appears. *Eventually* the numbers average out.

It Is Easy to Quit

Make no mistake, it is *hard* to keep going when it doesn't look like anything is happening (i.e., there are no results). I used to say to Steve, "I'm knocking on all these doors, talking to all these people, and nothing is happening." His reply was always, "How do you know?" Yeah, how *do* I really know that nothing is happening? The Universe is all connected. We are all vibrating bundles of energy. How do we know "how" it's all connected? The answer, I learned, was that the "how" is none of my business. Here's how it finally sank in.

"The 'how' is none of your business."
—Steve Shull

After my second year in Colorado, I began to notice that when July came around, it was hot (duh), and there would be fewer people home while I was at the doors. That was frustrating, because I am out there sweating and working my butt off and talking to fewer people. Then one day, while sitting in a Starbucks, I was listening to people talk: "Hey, where have you been?" The answer: "We've been away." I listened more and more over the next few weeks, and then it hit me: people take vacation in July! This is especially true in the suburbs, where lots of people have kids. School starts again in early to mid-August, so July is when many people take time off. Which got me thinking: I might as well take a little time off too.

In July of 2011, I was finally beginning to make some headway growing my business again (remember, I had left California at the end of 2008 and started all over again in the beginning of 2009). The first two years were excruciatingly difficult, both personally and professionally. Now I was finally starting to get things squared away and beginning to get a little bit of traction. In the prior two years, I had worked nonstop through the summer, but this year I took off some time in early July.

While it was nice to take a break from the heat, I was feeling a little guilty. I decided in mid-July that August was going to be a big push: I created the "August 5000," where I was going to knock on 5,000 doors in the month of August. I had never even come close to something like that. I laid out a plan, organized my schedule, and started on August 1.

A couple of notes here: First, I told people, which created an extra layer of accountability. I told my vendors, and I told some of my clients. Second, August 2011 turned out to be one of the hottest Augusts on record in Colorado. As the month began: five days in, five straight days of 90-plus degree heat at 5,900 feet of altitude, I already felt like quitting. However, on day six, a couple people called me and said, "Hey, how's it going?" S#*$. Now I can't quit. Too many people know that I am doing this. I have to go all the way to the end.

Things are not always directly related, nor do they happen instantaneously.

When the month ended, I was at 4,600 doors. I didn't get to 5,000. Was I disappointed? No way. It really wasn't about "5,000" doors. It was about pushing myself way out of my comfort zone. It really took something for me to do that. When it was over, I told myself: "F*#@ that, I am never doing that again!" It was sooooo hard.

When I tell the story of the August 5,000, people always ask, "How many deals did you do from that?" The answer is, "Zero." I did zero deals over the next five months directly from any of those doors. In fact, the very next deal came from what is called "head knocking."

One day, in the middle of that August, I went to go pick up my daughter from ballet class. It was around 4 p.m., and I was hot, sweaty, and tired. I came into the facility a few minutes early and sat down next to one of the moms. We started talking, and a week later I was showing her and her husband houses. My very next sale in the middle of all this door-knocking activity did not come directly from the doors—and neither did the next few sales. However, at the beginning of 2012, five sales came directly from those doors in August. Things are not always directly related, nor do they happen instantaneously.

The point is to be in action. We do not know how everything is connected. We have no idea how it is actually going to turn out—like who our next client will be. If we can stay focused on our process, stay in right-action, the odds go up dramatically that good things will eventually happen.

It's hard to keep going.

Resistance would like us to move on to something else. Resistance wants us to second-guess ourselves, to lull us into believing that we are on the wrong track. Many people look at the doors and say that it is a complete waste of activity. I say that they are looking on the surface. They—we—don't see how it is all connected. Mostly, I believe that this is because we think it is easier to move on to something else. It is easy to "try" knocking on doors (or any lead generation method) for six weeks, not see direct results, and then say, "Aw, this doesn't work," and move on to something else. That is what is easy. Doing what is hard: To persevere. To stick with something that isn't easy, something that isn't giving us instant gratification. That is hard.

We have a choice—do what is easy, or do what is hard.

Look, it isn't easy. It is hard to stick with something. Professor and author of *Grit*, Angela Duckworth says that "sticking with things over the very long term until you master them" is her definition of grit. "The gritty individual approaches achievement as a marathon; his or her advantage is stamina."

She also talks about perseverance and passion. I don't consider myself very passionate, and I rate my perseverance as pretty average. It *is* hard to keep going. It is hard to stay present to your *why* (if you had clarified one), it is hard to define your most important thing, then block everything out except that one thing. It is difficult to keep going with no 'instant gratification'. That is the path, and it is simple but not easy. There will always be speed bumps along the way. It's okay if they slow you down from time to time, just don't let them take you out.

A Couple of Words on Momentum

Just because the world's innovations are happening faster and faster does not mean that everything we want gets created quicker. Back to the movie *Pretty Woman*: There were a couple of scenes where Richard Gere is talking on a mobile phone—which was almost the size of a wine bottle. The only task it performed was phone calls. No texting, no web surfing, no email, no apps. Think about how long it took to get from there to where we are now. It is a progression.

I have a friend that started in real estate a few years before me. When I met her in 2006, I remember her saying that her goal was to sell 50 homes a year. She was selling maybe 12–24 homes per year, and fluctuated in that range. Then, she moved up to 20–30 homes per year. By 2012, she finally hit 50. By 2019, she and her team were selling over 200 homes per year, with a 25% market share in their primary farm city of 8,000-plus homes. She is highly competent and intelligent—and—she worked her tail off. It still took time for it to build upon itself. She never ever stopped. She never ever switched tactics. It was door knocking and open house. Did she do some marketing along the way? Sure. Did she have speed bumps to overcome? Of course. The more momentum that she built, the more she stuck with what worked, which cycled back into the more momentum that she built. I watched her build her business, even when I had moved away to Colorado. Fifty homes seemed almost impossible when she was at 20. When she got to 50, the goal became 100. A hundred homes in a year seemed ridiculous. Reading this now, it does not seem that way. When we are starting somewhere and we look at where we want to go, the gap often seems overwhelming. As we start the journey, it does not feel like we are making any progress. However, the more that we stay in motion, the more that we keep on going, the more that the momentum works in our favor.

As Darren Hardy explains in the *Compound Effect*, our efforts, if they are the right efforts and they are done consistently over time, compound. Our retirement account exponentially expands the longer it is compounding interest. The more homes that we sell, the more our signs are in the yards, the more people get to know us, the more our business expands. It doesn't happen on day one. It compounds. Which, by definition, means *over time*!

The Journey Is the Reward

The reward is not selling more homes. The reward is not cashing the commission check. Those are nice, but they are a result. They are a result of what happens when we repeatedly do what we are supposed to do.

The sales come and go, as do the commission checks. Sometimes we have more of them, sometimes we have fewer of them. We have no control over the result. None. Zero. There is nothing that we can do today that will absolutely make a sale. We can, however, follow our process, which we have absolute control over. We can win every day by a function of following our process. Therefore, if we want to be attached to something, we can be attached to our process—be attached to doing what we said we would do and then doing it.

I never ever feel like knocking on doors. Never. I love having done it. I love having met people. I love having walked, outside, in the sunshine. I love having knocked on 125,000+ doors, met tens of thousands of people, and learned so many personal stories and experiences that I have long lost count.

To me, the process of being in my business, the certainty it can give to me, is my reward. I don't have to spend any mental anxiety worrying or wondering. I don't have to get caught up with how many sales I make. I only have to worry about one thing: did I knock on doors today?

Which brings me back to this ultimate realization: the journey is the reward. All this talk about results, sales, money—it is all temporary. We sell 30 homes this year, and next year we start again at zero. We could have sold 30-plus homes per year for 20 years, over 600 homes, and when the new year starts we are right back at zero. Past results do not matter—at least in terms of creating results this year.

What we are faced with is the journey. The journey of the week, the month, the quarter, the year, our career. It is ongoing, ever-changing, like a river. It bends, it flows, sometimes quite forcefully, other times it slows to a trickle. The key is to keep flowing.

8

COMPARISON IS THE
THIEF OF OUR JOY

It's not just about whether we think we can or can't—it is about all the things that we debate and doubt within ourselves. Are we good enough? Are we smart enough? Are we pretty enough? Are we as successful as that person? Sometimes we make statements such as: I will never be as _____ as that person. That person is so _____, I will never be as good as them.

"Whether you think you can, or you think you can't—you're right."
—Henry Ford

One of the most insidious, destructive conversations that we have with ourselves is that of comparison and judgement. It is fundamentally human nature to compare. Not being aware of the tendency though can jeopardize our overall fulfillment and satisfaction.

Living a life that is fulfilled, joyous, loving, grati-
fying, expressed—that is, experiencing these ways of
being throughout our days—I am asserting that this
is the ultimate reward. We could say that our life is
fulfilled through ways of being, because . . . we are
human *beings*, not human doings. We don't have to
"do" anything to experience life this way, because
they are created, and they are created regardless
of circumstances. Yet, as real estate agents, we are
constantly reminded by those around us. We look
at how everyone else is doing, comparing ourselves
to them. We forget that in those moments we are
robbing our own fulfillment, expression, and joy by
looking externally for some sort of validation.

Comparison *is* the thief of our joy. Comparing
ourselves to others is undermining our aliveness
and enjoyment of the present. We may question
ourselves with thoughts like: Am I really any good?
How did they get that buyer/listing? Why didn't
I get that business? We start with this comparing,
which completely disempowers us, and right behind
it is doubt. The lack of belief that we are smart
enough, good enough, worthy enough. We look at
others and think that maybe they know something
that we don't. Maybe they have something that we
don't. Maybe I won't be any good at this. Maybe my
time has come to hang it up. For me, these spiraling
thoughts are completely disempowering and have
cracked my belief over the years. Belief in what?
Belief in myself.

Dealing with Comparison

Of all the things that I have done in my life, I cannot think of one area that is more challenging than real estate. With well over one million realtors, there is no shortage of opportunities for us to compare ourselves to others.

- *In our office:* Consider any time that we have walked into the office and looked at the "sales board." We look, and we see our peers with several sales. Now, maybe our name is up there, maybe it isn't. If it isn't, we think, "*Crap, I suck, I am never going to get up there,*" or "*This is lame, I don't understand why I don't have more sales,*" or "*I hate feeling this way, so I won't ever look again.*" Maybe our name is up there—we are having an active year, or month, and yet we still look up there and see someone else who is doing more. We think that we are better than them, or work harder than them, yet there they are—ahead of us on the board. We completely invalidate our accomplishment by focusing on what other people are doing.

- *In our market:* Perhaps we compete with one or two specific agents in a geographic area. Or maybe we just run across a few agents repeatedly. Or maybe they are just the agents touted as "number one." We might say, "*Oh, it was given to them . . . their parents, and now they are well con-*

nected and living off those connections."
Or, *"They're such jerks, I would never want
to be someone like that. I would rather do
no business than that kind of business."* Or,
*"They are so amazing, I could never be as
good as them. I should just quit now."*

- <u>*In our city or across the country:*</u> If we live
in a big market or small market. If we sell on
the high end or low end. Whichever end of
those spectrums we are on, we look at the
other side and think, "It's better over there."
For example, if you work the high end,
when it's good, it's *really* good. But when
it's bad, it's *really* bad. On the bad cycles,
we think, "We should just do the lower end
stuff that always sells." If we do the low(er)
end, we think, "Those agents on the high
end have it so easy—they can sell just a few
houses and make more than I do selling 20
or 30!" If we live in a big market, we could
say that there is too much competition, we
should go somewhere smaller. If we live in
a smaller market, we say that we should go
to a bigger market because a small market
is too stifling—there's not enough opportunity because everyone knows each other.

Why stop there? We could also compare across
the following:

- <u>Out-of-area agents:</u> If we work a geographic
area, inevitably an agent comes in, takes

a listing, then lists the two other homes around it. We say, "It's not fair!"

- Gender: Men have it easier / Women have it easier.

- Age: Older people think that the younger people have it so easy because they are tech savvy, they can do more online marketing, and youth is sexier. Younger people think that it's not fair that people don't take them seriously, or that all the older people have more connections, or that you have to have experience to get more experience.

The world is big; does it really make sense to be in competition with the entire populace? By the way, if your "comparison" isn't listed, you can fill it in now.

Comparison is a lose-lose scenario.

After reading through all these comparisons, what are you left with? To me, it's draining, disempowering, and flat-out exhausting.

Hopefully what you can also see: it is a total waste of time! Our ego/mind can always find a way to justify the other person's seeming advantage! Most importantly, IT IS MADE UP! None of these things is true except in our own head. For every person reading this chapter, they will have a different experience regarding comparison and doubt. I am asserting that all of us can point to some scenario where we have disempowered ourselves through comparing.

Judgement

The previous chapter dealt with developing patience and settling into the journey. Before that, we talked about all the distractions that take us off course. Here, we are taking another look at the more subtle nuances of Resistance: comparison, judgement, lack of belief—all of those things are us sabotaging ourselves.

One way this type of sabotage showed up for me: when I look at someone else and say they have an "-er," like: better, easier, prettier, smarter, taller, shorter, faster, slower, calmer, funnier... Was it true? Were those other people better than me? Don't know. Probably not in all areas. And, it doesn't matter! There will always be someone who is better/richer/taller/prettier than us. So, playing that game is a lose-lose scenario.

Instead, it takes real courage to stop, look within, and believe in ourselves. Believe that we are enough. Believe that we are on the right path. Believe that it will all work out.

I cannot tell you how many times that I have been taken out by comparison and judgement. I cannot tell you how many times I have gone out to the doors in the summer when the high-altitude sun is beating down and I'm sweating my butt off and nothing seems to be happening in my business. Yet when I look around, it sure *seems* like "everyone else" has it easy because their business is "just magically coming to them." I cannot tell you how many times I have gone to an office meeting, or any other group of my peers, and it looks like *everyone* is doing way better than me. In the moment, it feels like I am a fraud. It feels like I am wasting my time. It feels like I am doing it wrong. Every. Single. Time. It never went away. It always seems like everyone else is cruising along with no speed bumps.

They are not, of course. What I have realized is that *everyone* has struggles, because everyone is human. When I talk to agents one-on-one, and we look under the façade, we are all alike. We all have crap to deal with. We all have struggle, we all have doubt—that's part of being human. Some people deal with it better than others, but it is a skill that we all can learn. However, the very first step is acknowledging that it is there. We can stop pretending that it doesn't exist.

So, that left me with a choice: keep doubting what I was doing, sabotaging myself along the way, or settle in and keep going. I did not need to worry about what everyone else was doing. My process worked. My process gave me stability and certainty. I finally did believe that in the end it was all going to work out. As Henry Ford said, either way I am right. I had to constantly remind myself: Selling real estate is not anything new—I am doing what has already been proven to work for decades. I am not inventing the next iPhone—I am selling real estate. How do we succeed in real estate? Talk to people.

Failure

Does the fear of failure and rejection ever go away? No. You *can* change your context, though.

One spring day in 2007, I took an agent with me to go door knocking. She wanted to see what I did and how it worked. Sure, I said, and under three conditions:

1. Wear comfortable shoes.
2. Don't say anything (i.e., no talking while we are out walking and knocking).
3. Stay out of my way (meaning, don't stand in the way of me walking to and from the doors).

She agreed. She met me in a neighborhood, and out we went. True to her word, she didn't say anything. She patiently followed me from house to house, from door to door, and did exactly as she promised. After about an hour, we made it back to our cars for a quick break, some water, and a little debriefing.

As we approached the car, she blurted out, *"How can you stand all that rejection!!!???"*

Huh? I was taken aback. I really had no idea what she was talking about. To me, we had knocked on 30 or more doors, spoke with about eight or 10 people, a couple of which we had some engaging conversations with. No one was moving, but they were respectful, kind, and interesting.

At that moment, I realized that, implicitly, I had developed three intentions at the door:

1. Leave people better off than when I found them,

2. Look for a "now" real estate opportunity, and

3. Be of service.

The odds of someone moving the day that I knock on their door is low. Disappointingly low. If I only looked at the doors as a win-or-lose situation based on someone needing me to help them move, it would be constant "rejection." Instead, I can win at every door. I can smile. I can wish them well. I can listen and be of service. Now, that doesn't mean that I am there to pander or insert myself with distracting or unnecessary situations in people's lives, but it does mean that how we frame the situation makes a huge difference. There was not failure and rejection at the door. There was in the beginning, but once I reframed the context in which I operated, failure at the door did not exist.

Does the fear of failure and rejection ever go away? No.

Look, I still had three kids to feed. I *had* to find people who wanted to buy and sell homes. To say that there weren't years that were not so good— yes, those to me were failures. But not at the doors. There was no real failure at the door. The only failure at the door came from me not being my best in that moment, maybe too scared to press a little further with someone, maybe a little too scared to ask one final question—those were actions that I could have taken and didn't. That had nothing to do with the person I was speaking with. It had to do with me not being more courageous. If someone was moving and it wasn't with me—which did/does happen, that's not a failure. That means they prefer to work with someone else, and I can choose not to take that personally. Some people want to work with me, some don't. My job: find more people who want to work with me.

Lack

It is so easy to get hijacked into comparison when we are coming from a place where something is missing, especially when the something that is missing is very much needed—like income. When our sales are down and our expenses are up, we can experience a lot of stress and anxiety. When we see other people seemingly doing well while we are not, it can exacerbate the feeling of lack.

The first half of 2018 was not my best year. In fact, it was one of my hardest times. I was certainly not new in the business, and I wasn't new to town. I was established and one of those people who "should be" doing well in what was still a very good market, in the busiest time of the year. But not much was happening.

One of my clients referred me to a family that needed to buy a home. We started working together, and right away we wrote an offer on a property in multiple offers and lost. They had narrowed down their search to a specific neighborhood where nothing was for sale. I asked them if they would like me to go door-to-door to find them a house, which they agreed to, so off I went. After a couple of days, I had a couple of leads on some interesting properties. I called the buyer, Rob (name changed), and I didn't hear from him. I didn't hear from him for almost a week. That was odd.

When Rob finally called me back, he said that they were busy and had been driving around, but nothing serious. They said to hold off on that neighborhood because they were rethinking their plans. He said to check back with him in a week or so.

A week goes by, I call him back, and he says sorrowfully, "Hey, um, we bought a new build and we close in a couple days."

Are you f@#$%*g kidding me? Seriously?

Meanwhile, at about the same time, I have another client, Gary (name changed), who had been increasing his motivation to move. I had known Gary for many years from the doors, and we had become very friendly. We had looked at a few properties over the years, but either it wasn't the right time or wasn't the right property. Now he said that he was a little more serious.

Background: In the neighborhoods that I knock regularly, I have a search set up for each one. Every morning, I receive an email with any changes in the neighborhood, new listings, under contracts, and solds. Two weeks after my conversation with Gary, I open my email and there is an email alert from his neighborhood. One of the new listings is Gary's house! *"What the ____!?!?"* I don't call him—I am beyond upset.

Two days later, I am in Los Angeles for a training. It's 8 a.m. Pacific time, and I am standing with a group of friends, catching up before the event starts.

My phone rings; I can see that it's Gary. I excuse myself and step away to answer the phone. I answer the call with "Hello." That is all I said. Gary's immediate reply was—and I am not making this up, "*I f@#*&?% up.*" He proceeded to tell me how he got snookered into working with this other agent, and how she had "pressured him" to list his house with her. He felt terrible, and he was calling to apologize.

Now, if this is happening to us agents when we are in the middle of a very busy quarter, these things bounce off of us pretty easily. But when things are not going so good and we are feeling scarcity creep in, then letting these balls bounce off us is much harder. This is exactly the moment when this business can take people out. Even if we recover with more sales (which, of course, we all can do), there is some piece of us that sometimes hangs on to these upsets. We take it personally. We become jaded. We hold grudges. Maybe against our clients, against the business, or maybe even ourselves.

Important to note: What did make a difference to me was that he was willing to call. He honored the relationship and made what was likely a very difficult call for him.

Where did that leave me? Not any richer. I really "needed" that sale. When I stepped away from this place of lack and scarcity, I realized that this was a breakthrough. He didn't really "owe me" anything. The fact that he honored a relationship, a relationship that was created out of nothing, was very inspiring. I am just a middle-aged, balding guy who knocks on doors, yet I finally could see that I create relationships with people that mean something. Sure, it would have been nicer to sell his house, but was there a bigger message here?

You Can Only Quit at the End

"The career I have chosen is laden with opportunity yet it is fraught with heartbreak and despair and the bodies of those who have failed, were they piled one atop another, would cast a shadow down upon all the pyramids of the earth."
— Og Mandino, *The Greatest Salesman in the World*

If we took Mr. Mandino's quote and applied it to the piles of discarded real estate licenses, we could tape them all together and probably go to the moon and back. I am reminded by another Fred'ism (Fred Wilson, a longtime, top-producing agent in La Quinta, California, and one of my early mentors), *"Then there are those agents that quit but stay."* He was referring to the agents who give up on achieving their goals and dreams, never living up to their full potential, but they don't actually turn in their license—they sort of just hang around.

Today's glamour and success that is portrayed on HGTV, Bravo, and other media sources for the allure of selling high-end real estate is deceiving. First off, that is all for show. Second, only so few succeed at that level. Seems like we are back to that 80/20 thing . . .

In 2000, I did a nine-month leadership course with about 125 other people. It was another of those hard things. It was the best training that I have ever done. It was co-led by three people who alternated leading sessions and weekends. One of the leaders was this extraordinary woman named Candace. I remember that, at the very beginning, she said in her Arkansas drawl, "This course is like a roller coaster. I don't recommend gettin' off in the middle of the ride. If you wanta get off, you gotta make it to the end."

In retrospect, I think *everyone* at some point wanted to quit. Some did. Some quit but stayed. Unlike real estate, there was a high level of accountability, there were course leaders, coaches, accountability partners. There was no place to hide, and if you "went missing," there were people calling and checking up on you. That is not true in real estate. People go missing all the time. People disappear for months, sometimes years!

No matter how bad things got, nor how difficult times were, I knew that I couldn't get off this real estate ride. Not just because I didn't "have a Plan B," but because I hadn't gotten to the end yet. As I have written in this book, I have experienced struggle in my real estate career. I knew that I could do better. I knew I wasn't at the end. I knew that I could achieve "more." More what though? More sales? More money? For me, I love training and coaching. I love helping people break through to what's next. So getting to this place was important, not figuring out how to make a million dollars.

If you don't have an end in sight for you, would it be a bad idea to come up with one? The best example I have comes not from within real estate, but from someone in the speaking industry that I will refer to as Lisa. She related that early in her speaking career she had figured out what would be "enough." She came up with a plan so that when she hit a certain level in terms of income and assets, she could pull back the throttles. It was very specific. When she hit that number, she *actually* pulled back. She only said yes to things that she absolutely wanted to do. She only said yes to clients who were willing to hire her on her terms.

This example is so telling because (a) it is universal—this concept is not unique to just real estate; (b) it shows that clear thinking up front laid the path for what was to follow; (c) it happened over time—she didn't get what she created in year one (or year two, five, or 10!); and (d) she did it. When she got to the end, she actually did what she set out to do—pull back the reins. Lisa did not stay on the hamster wheel.

You don't have to have her goal. You may always want to go at it full bore—totally fine. The point is to be clear about what works for you, and be conscious of the choice that you made.

9

DEVELOPING GRATITUDE AND APPRECIATION

My Gratitude Journey

Gratitude is not a new thing. It feels new(er) to me because I had no education or instruction in practicing gratitude until my late thirties to early forties.

"Reflect upon your present blessings of which every man has many—not on your past misfortunes, of which all men have some."
— *Charles Dickens*

I first read (per Steve's coaching) *The Science of Getting Rich* (abbreviated as TSOGR), by Wallace D. Wattles, in 2006, although it was published in 1910. About the same time that I discovered TSOGR, the book and movie *The Secret* had come out. TSOGR did not have any of the hoopla and fanfare nor any of the notoriety and publicity of *The Secret*. Nothing against *The Secret*—I got a lot out of it, and the book remains on my bookshelf. However, I refer back to TSOGR many times throughout each year. One chapter that I come back to often is the one titled "Gratitude,"—in fact, it is the book's longest chapter.

In hindsight, it occurred to me that I had no real appreciation or practice of gratitude until mid-2018. That seems crazy to me because I "felt" like I appreciated people, and was good at expressing appreciation and acknowledgement of others. What was missing, I realized, was the *practice* of gratitude. Feeling a deep sense of appreciation from within. Appreciation for what? For everything that I had, but more importantly, everything that I did not.

For most of my real estate career, and probably my life, I was always trying to get somewhere. I was always trying to "make it." This was absolutely the case in real estate. To have X number of transactions, to have sold X dollars, so that I had lots of money to demonstrate that "I made it." The money wasn't really what I wanted. What I really wanted was to work as little as possible, make enough to live my life, and hang out with my family. Yet I felt the "should" pressure to sell at a certain threshold for validation and self-worth. For the last several years, my self-image as a speaker and trainer was also caught up in "how many homes I sold."

Back to mid-2018: It was not going so well. As mentioned in a previous chapter, a few clients went AWOL on me and there was a bit of a dry spell. The lack of business just created more stress, anxiety, and worst of all, depression. I was severely depressed.

Getting my body and mind in a state of feeling good was exactly what was missing, because in order to create an external world that made me feel good, it started with creating it internally first.

Conceptually I knew this, but I was not doing it. I had all these financial commitments: my daughter was supposed to go to a Joffrey Ballet intensive ($$$), I was supposed to take my oldest son on a college tour out of state ($), and my partner and I had booked (the previous December) a week in Europe during the second week of July ($$). However, by May of 2018, I was completely freaking out over realities like: little business, dwindling cash reserves, and lots of obligations.

Family offered to front the money for my daughter. The trip with my son was a road trip, so that wasn't going to cost very much. I still had the trip to Europe though, and I did not really have the money required for that trip. Nor did I feel that it had any integrity for me to go on that type of vacation while I was in a stressed financial position. My domestic partner was adamant: not going on the trip was not an option. She was going to pay for the trip—everything, and I could pay her back whenever. In fact, she said, "Don't pay me back, just cover the next trip."

Off we went to London and Amsterdam for a week. It was amazing, and, true to her word, she graciously paid for everything. Believe it or not, being "taken care of" for a week was incredibly difficult. It took a lot of mental work to be in the moment, enjoy the gift that was given to me, and not judge myself for having been in that spot financially. The trip itself was incredible. The point is not about the highlights of the trip, it was what I learned from the experience. I first had to surrender. What there was for me to get: not being attached, not having things have to be a specific way, and not having to be in control. I learned about not knowing how it is all going to work out in the end. That week was about letting someone else contribute to me, creating a new experience for no other reason than because she loved and appreciated me. It provided an experience of companionship, partnership, and contribution.

When we returned from the trip and I got back into my work routine, something shifted in my early morning journaling and meditation. I began to be grateful for everything. It started with the gift of that week, plus all the other amazing things I had in my life: my kids, my parents, my friends, my business associates, my clients. I was grateful for all the people at the doors. For all the people that came to my classes. For my firm. For my mentors. For my coach. Then, all the other details throughout my day gave me a whole other sense of appreciation. Seeing a sunrise. Seeing a sunset. Watching and hearing it rain. *Spending time* with my kids. Drinking coffee in the morning. Having healthy food in my refrigerator and pantry. For the wisdom that I heard on podcasts, and for what I learned from all the books that I was reading. Every day, I realized that there was so much to be grateful for. In fact, I saw for the first time that I had more than I ever needed. Way more.

The more grateful I became, the more inner peace I had. The absolute joy and appreciation for my family. The time that I spent with my kids on Sunday mornings, having brunch and goofing around. Having my oldest son wanting to hang out with me instead of his friends (not all the time, of course, but many times). Having clients who were loyal, apprecia-tive, and fun. My transac-tions always flowed with grace and ease, even when there was a problem that came up. My life works and flows with abundance.

"He is a wise man who does not grieve for the things which he has not, but rejoices for those which he has."
— *Epictetus*

It was all there before, I just never really saw it. I was always focused on where I "should be," because what was in the way was all the "striving for." I already had an amazing life—I just wasn't being thankful and appreciative of it. So what if I had a little less money from time to time than some of my peers? So what if I wasn't the number-one agent in the office? I was on this incredible journey. I found a whole new appreciation in the doors, because every single day I had the opportunity to come into more physical contact with other human beings than most other agents (and most people). The breadth of my expe-rience was wide because of the doors—the neigh-borhoods I knocked, the people I met with whom I became friends—and my wide range of real estate clients, coaching clients, and peers in mastermind and coaching groups.

At the doors, when someone does stop to talk to me at the door, it usually goes one of two ways. The first is casual and brief—they often thank me for stopping by, and that's it. The other is the exact opposite. People stop what they are doing and, for a few minutes, engage in a different kind of conversation, the nature of which often leads to more reflection and introspection. They are commenting on why they live where they live, where—if anywhere else—would they live, and why. Remember, I am catching people at their most cherished place: their home. Every day begins and ends right where we are standing. This is the place they raised/are raising their family, where they host celebrations and holidays.

It is not uncommon for people to get into all the areas of what's happening in their life. Not everyone's life is filled with only good memories. We all have times in our lives that aren't all roses and rainbows. Regardless, in these conversations I am creating a space where people open up and share about what's happened/happening and what their future looks like. I personally find this a remarkable and amazing privilege.

It is a culmination of these experiences in mid-2018 that I think had me appreciate all that I already had. That's not to say that I am not creating new experiences and outcomes, but it starts with the fact that I can appreciate all that I already had. The doors had been a huge gift I was dismissing.

I remember an explanation of gratitude from one of the top agents in Southern California. He was sharing how he sees gratitude and God/the

Universe/Spirit working together. He basically said: "Pretend that you give someone a present. If they don't appreciate the present; if they just toss it off to the side, how likely are you to give them another present? Not likely. The Universe works the same way. It is giving us things all the time. If we are tossing them behind us and saying, "That isn't what I wanted, give me something else," we are going to be disappointed because probably nothing else is coming. The Universe, like us, only gives presents to people who appreciate them. All of the presents, not just the fancy ones."

I could clearly see what had been missing: true appreciation for where I was and where I wasn't; and for what I had and what I had not.

I could clearly see what had been missing: true appreciation for where I was and where I wasn't; and for what I had and what I had not.

A Different Perspective

French novelist Marcel Proust famously said that the real voyage of discovery *"consists not in seeking new landscapes, but in having new eyes."*

A funny thing about the doors: I see things that otherwise get missed. The one thing that is consistent when I am walking through a neighborhood: it is slow. I am not in a car. I am not on a bike. I am not on a scooter. I am walking. This gives me plenty of time to look around and see things. I am not on my phone. I am not searching the internet. I am not texting people. I am not doing anything but walking from house to house and talking to people. There is no other reason to be there. If I am going to be there, then I really need to *be* there.

As we discussed in a previous chapter, being present is difficult. We are constantly being distracted. We are constantly busy being busy. We are constantly in our heads, worrying, thinking, judging, etc. But being present, being available, actively listening and experiencing—takes practice. That is one of the other many gifts of the doors that I am grateful for—the opportunity to be distraction-free. The opportunity to put myself in a space where there is nothing else to do but go "be with" people.

When I did the "August 5,000" I was in a hurry. I needed to get to 200-plus doors per day. In retrospect, the goal was not necessarily about business, or connecting to people, it was about hitting a number. Sure, it was challenging, and I learned things about myself in the process. However, the real point of knocking on doors had been pushed aside. The real point is to connect with people.

The other benefit of knocking on doors is the experience and knowledge that can be gained in no other manner. Learning who lives in the neighborhood, what's on people's minds, what's in their plans, why people move into the neighborhood, why they move out, and why they stay. I now could see and appreciate all of it.

What's the Rush?

When I am driving my car, I am always in a rush—even when I am not in a hurry. I just *have* to get around people, I feel that I have to go at my own pace. In other areas of my life, I am almost never in a hurry. The opportunity to be in the moment, to experience what is going on—that is the real gift. If we are always rushing, where do we end up? Seriously, if we look back on the last week, or last month, and we can picture ourselves "rushing," where did we end up? Didn't we end up exactly where we did? The experience of rushing didn't do anything except take us out of the present moment.

Several years ago, I was on a group coaching call and someone was talking about how busy they were, and they didn't have enough time to prospect. So, they just rushed right through their prospecting, going as fast as they could. Steve was leading that call and he replied, "What's the rush? Where are you hurrying to?" Hmmmm . . . wow. I sort of implicitly knew that to be the case, but I never had taken the time to put some thought into it. Being an observer in someone else's situation gave me another insight. It gave me permission to go even slower at the doors. Take more time with the right people. When I was with someone at the door, I was *with* them. I was not thinking about what else I had going on, where I had to be next, or how many doors I was not getting to while I was talking to them. I was simply being with them in the moment. I began to put less focus on the number of doors that I knocked on, and more focus on improving my ability to be present with people.

Having a target goal of doors and people spoken to is important, especially for people who are establishing the habit. At some point for me, the habit had long been ingrained, and now it was about going deeper (that progression thing again).

I believe that the connections I made with people, the selfies (the pictures I took with people at the door), all came from going slowly. From being present. From being grateful for the opportunity to be with someone face-to-face, engaged in a conversation. I was never looking to "get" anything from people.

Giving vs. Getting

When I read Bob Burg and John David Mann's *The Go-Giver*, I thought, "Aha! Finally, someone validating what I have been doing at the doors!" That was not exactly the intention of the book—to validate Steven Ross's door knocking—however, it was another external validation of what I knew to be the right thing. I always felt that when I was at the door, I was there to serve people. Of course, I still needed to sell real estate. I also knew that the odds of someone needing to move the moment that I knocked on the door were very low. Therefore, if door knocking were going to work for me, it had to be about "them"—the people opening the doors. I had to be there to serve *them*.

I highly recommend *The Go-Giver,* it is a quick and easy read—and worth your time. The authors detail the Five Laws of Stratospheric Success:

(1) Value, (2) Compensation, (3) Influence, (4) Authenticity, and (5) Receptivity. For me, the book has three implications that I would like to touch upon (the laws 1, 3, and 4), and more specifically, how they applied to me most in terms of what I was doing at the doors.

The Law of Value talks about giving more than receiving. I am not receiving any payment at the door. Zero. Therefore anything I "give" to people outweighs what I receive in payment. What was I giving at the door? My time. Sure, I handed out information that provided data and insight into the market. Mostly though, I was giving my listening and compassion.

The third law, that of Influence, says that our impact is a function of how well we place other people's interests first. As a fiduciary for our clients, a realtor's primary function is putting the client's interests first. Always. When the public talks about bad experiences with real estate agents, I am asserting that it is often because they felt the agent was not on their side, and that the fiduciary duty was breached. In other words, the clients felt that the agent was doing what was best for the agent, not the clients. At the doors, I am only there to serve the person in front of whom I am standing, which means that if they don't want to talk/can't talk, then the thing to do is get out of their way. However, if they don't mind talking, then whatever is on their mind is what's worth talking about (most of the time).

Owning that the most valuable gift to give is ourselves, *The Law of Authenticity* was the hardest for me to get. Maybe other people have that one handled, but it really took a long time to get to the place where that was true for me: all I had to give was myself. Putting my attention on someone else; offering a piece of advice, insight, or information that to me is obvious, but to another, it can seem like a breakthrough.

More recently, I was making my way through a neighborhood that I had knocked for quite some time. I came to Ellen's door, where we had chatted many times over the years. She was probably not ever moving, and honestly, I am not sure if she did that she would call me—simply because her kids might be more influential in the process (and I have never met her kids). Nevertheless, when I got to her house this day, she came to the door thrilled to see me. After brief greetings, she had a real estate question. She was trying to help her son out with a condo, and she wasn't sure what to do. Should she use her cash to help lower his payment, how does that work, etc.? I asked her a few questions and presented a couple of scenarios, all of which were obvious to me but not to her. She now saw some options that she had not seen before. This was an issue that had been stressing her out for the last few months. Now in a matter of minutes, she had a couple of solutions that completely alleviated her stress. As I was leaving, she profusely thanked me, with tears in her eyes. All I did was stop by, on my usual rounds, and be of service.

How Much Is Enough?

Diogenes inscribed a line from Epicurus on a wall in Turkey: *"He who is not satisfied with a little is satisfied with nothing."*

If you are reading this book, then you have made it. You are not starving. You have a roof over your head. Maybe we have had some tough(er) times in our lives, but overall, we have made it. So, how much is "enough"?

Many studies around the world have shown that, beyond a basic level, more money does not increase well-being. In the United States, the cutoff is said to be about $75,000. If you live in Los Angeles, San Francisco, or New York—maybe it's more (even where I live in Denver has gotten pretty expensive). Let's say $150,000. Would it be unfair to say that there is *some* number, between $75,000 and $150,000, that more than covers our basic needs? That anything beyond that is not making us any happier?

Look, in full disclosure, I like nice stuff. I love nice clothes, nice shoes, and driving a new car every two years. I love traveling. I love staying in nice hotels. I love taking my kids skiing, and taking them on trips. All of those things cost money. But at some point, what is making me happier? One more night in a Four Seasons? Another brand name pair of jeans? Another pair of fancy sneakers?

Probably not. If I am being honest, as much as I like nice things, I have the most joy and fulfillment when I am spending time with the closest people in my life. For most of the past 10 years, it has been with my children and my family (parents, siblings, cousins). Hands down. There isn't even a close second.

Which brings me back to the question, how much is enough? And, in line with the other questions of this chapter, what is all this for? What is the rush, what is the pull for more? More results, more money, more, more, more. There will always be more. We can always sell more homes. We can always make more money. When is enough . . . enough?

What I have right now is enough. Always.

Any time that I feel stress, angst, or this feeling of "more"—I know that is a trigger to remind myself to be grateful for what I have *right now*. For all that I have and all that I don't. What I have right now is enough. Always.

10

RESPONSIBILITY AND BEING AT PEACE

Most of us need a good night's sleep. We need restful, quiet sleep to rejuvenate and regenerate our energy; our cells repairing themselves from a hard day. You can look at your own experience and research to verify that this is the case—but that is not my main point.

There is also quite a bit of research around the darkness of the room, types of mattresses, and sleep positions that impact your sleep effectiveness. I am sure much of that is important, but that is not what I want to talk about either. Instead, consider the following:

> "A promise made from the stand that 'who you are is your word' engages you as participant. You cease to be spectator, and your words become actions that actually impact the world."
> — Werner Erhard

- What is your mind doing right before you go to bed?
- Did you just watch a movie?
- Were you watching or reading the news?
- Were you mindlessly surfing the internet?
- Were you lying there in bed ruminating over the day—particularly on things that might not have gone well, things that stress you out, or just otherwise cause restlessness? Things that you just can't let go?

I am neither a physician nor a sleep expert. However, the following phenomena has been my experience over my real estate career: every (working) day that I did what I was supposed to do—made my contacts via knocking on doors—that day was a success. Period. As we talked about, we are not in control of the results/outcome, only our actions. If we took the right action every day, then we did what we were supposed to do. Therefore, when I go to put my head on the pillow at night, I can be at peace. I can be at peace knowing that I did the most important thing to move my business, and my life, forward. I can also have a good night's sleep, regardless of my mattress, darkness in the room, and so on.

It really can be that simple.

In the realm of real estate, the most important thing every day was knocking on doors. If that one thing did not happen, my day was ruined—literally. It was the most important promise that I made to myself and my family, and if it got missed, it threw me off. I was definitely not at peace. No matter how amazing my day might have been, if door knocking got missed, I was "off." During the first 10 years of my real estate career, when I was still married, there were days when I would get home and, without me saying a word, my wife would look at me and say, "You didn't get to the doors today, did you?" She knew—I was that much of a jerk.

The number one key for me to go to bed at peace was to keep my word to myself. The number one promise I made: Go to the doors. That's it. Just get to the doors. Nothing great has to happen at the doors.

I am only in control of my actions, which includes my promises and fulfilling them.

I don't "have to get a lead" to make the day a success, all I had to do was the activity. I am not in control of the outcome, I am only in control of my actions, which includes my promises and fulfilling on them. Even when things were not rosy and abundant, I could go to bed every night at peace (or at least most nights) because I did the one thing that mattered most in my business: I knocked on doors.

Waking Up to Fall Asleep

You might be thinking, "If I don't do what I am supposed to do that day, then I can't go to bed peacefully?"

No, that is not what I am saying. What I am saying is that doing what we say—honoring our word, being responsible, being accountable —impacts our lives more than we might have been aware.

If we are still stirring about in our heads, playing over the injustices of the day, the things that made us upset, the things that didn't go right, the things that are worrying us and stressing us out— what is going to happen when we try to go to bed? Just because we lie down does not necessarily mean all that stuff goes away. It can, but it usually doesn't.

Honoring our word, being responsible, being accountable — impacts our lives more than we might have been aware.

We are the ones who are responsible for how our day went. If we want to end our day in peace, to end our day with grace and calm, we must be clear that it is we who say so. We need to be responsible for how the day went. What got done, what didn't get done, what things went right, what things did not go as planned. Also: What are we still hanging on to? What are we still upset about?

It is hard to be at peace when we are not complete with how the day went. By letting go of the day, even when it didn't go the way we wanted, we can put ourselves in a state of completion. In other words, we clean out the internal angst that prevents us from being at rest.

Start with Accountability

This whole book has been oriented around figuring out what is most important in your life and why, then designing your actions and an environment to fulfill upon them. We have dispensed with the idea of doing everything, and instead focusing only doing what is absolutely most important. We even talked about the universal force, Resistance, that is in your way. But in the end, we must still actually do the work day in and day out. How do we do that? *Accountability*—the word that most real estate agents never want to hear. We don't want to hear that word because it typically has a negative connotation. We got into real estate for "freedom and flexibility," and we think that being accountable gets in the way of that freedom. Here is a different way of looking at it: being accountable is simply the act of promising. "With a promise," Werner Erhard said, "you create a condition that supports your commitment rather than your moods."

As Steve said in the foreword, he has had his thumb in my back my entire real estate career. In a sense, I *always* had someone to answer to. I always had someone who cared, who was looking for me to fulfill what I was supposed to do every day. During the few times that I was "taking a break" from being accountable were the times that my actions (and results) went down—every time. Now, I am not saying that everyone should have a coach, or be in some sort of coaching program (although it *is* a good idea). I am saying that making promises and fulfilling on them has power. Think of the example of me doing the "August 5,000"—part of what kept me going is that I had told multiple people what I was doing—I was then "on the hook" to finish. I am sure that I would not have accomplished what I did without that extra layer of accountability.

That seems simple enough. But what happens when I miss? What happens when I don't fulfill my promise, or I don't do what I say? Isn't that really one of the main reasons that people don't want to promise? We don't want to promise because what if we don't do it?

Honor Our Word to Ourselves

In my late twenties I was introduced to the notion that our reality is shaped by our language. In other words, we are always speaking—first to ourselves, and then to others. If we stop for a moment and listen, what's happening? We are talking to ourselves. You might be saying to yourself, *"I'm not stopping right now, I need to finish reading this chapter. I am not telling myself anything. I have no idea what this guy is talking about."* Whatever is being said, it is being spoken in *language*.

What are we saying to ourselves? Are we beating ourselves up? Are we getting ourselves all riled up about some injustice that happened to us? Are we mad because of a client, or another agent? If we are still upset, are we having conversations to justify all that happened? All of these machinations are happening internally—we are having this ongoing conversation with ourselves. It's like a little dog yapping at us—*yap-yap-yap-yap-yap*, nonstop.

Going back to why we resist making promises: If we say we are going to do something, did we do it? I am going to work out. I am going to eat healthier. I am going to get more sleep. I am going to make those calls. And more. At the end of the day, did we do any of the things that we said we would do? It would be hard to fulfill these things when they are vague and not specific. Eat healthier—what does that mean? What does more sleep look like? Clearly we need to be specific. Going back to one of the first chapters, it's about getting clear on what's most important, and then being specific about what that looks like.

Let's look at the "be healthier" category that people often talk about. "Be healthier" isn't very specific, so let's say that we define it as exercising five days per week, and making all our weekday meals at home. The first day comes, and in our schedule at 7 a.m. it says, "Run three miles." Well, we slept in a little and missed that run. Next our schedule says, "7:45 to 8:00 a.m.—make lunch for the day," and that activity gets skipped for some other reason. Next thing we know, it's 2:15 p.m., we're starving, and we have an appointment at 2:30. We drive through a fast-food window, we scarf down something that's likely not supporting our "be healthier" commitment (and probably cost us more money). We didn't exercise, and we didn't prepare our food.

When we get to the end of the day, regardless of what else happened, here are two things that often get unacknowledged: We had said that we were going to do two things for our well-being, and we didn't do either one. Not only are those bad habits (not exercising and eating fast food), but more importantly, we aren't valuing the promises and commitments that we are making to ourselves. Our word and our promises have *no power*.

By the way, this works in all areas. When I was training for marathons, there was only one thing that I had to do: run. There were many days that I was not feeling well, or I was extra tired, or maybe I had trouble doing all the reps in a speed workout, or maybe I didn't run the exact mileage that I was supposed to at the exact pace. That didn't happen often, but as long as I still ran, it was a success. (I wasn't training to win Olympic gold, I was testing myself to see if I could do something hard.)

To say that we are going to do something and then do it, we are aligning the Universe in our favor. Like lining up dominos. The day looks and feels good when everything is aligned. If we miss an appointment or agreement, it's like taking a domino out of place. It just doesn't work the same. For many of us, we feel off, or out of alignment, and we don't know why. Sometimes it is as simple as we haven't been honoring/keeping our word to ourselves and others.

There is remarkable power in keeping our word to ourselves. If we can't keep it for ourselves, how in the world are we going to keep it with other people?

Giving Our Word to Others

If we say we are going to do something, are we doing what we said? Or are we constantly looking for a good explanation/justification for why we didn't do what we said we would do?

Going back to the example of being late: If we said that we are going to meet a client at 3:00 p.m., and we arrive at 3:05, we are late. If we can't honor our time commitments, what can we honor? Time, for me, is always a place to start. When I feel like my life isn't working, one of the first places I look: Am I on time? Am I getting up on time? Am I starting my workouts on time? Am I on time to my calls? My sales meeting? The doors? Any other appointments or promises? Then I look for all the other things that I said I would do and haven't done. These are usually the things in the background that I know that I said that I would do and haven't done. To make it worse, I haven't communicated to the person I committed to—I am just avoiding it. So, I haven't done what I said I would, and am avoiding dealing with the fact that I haven't done it—that's unsettling. This causes an inner angst. I find it very hard to go to bed at peace when there is angst—it's like trying to get rest when your stomach is upset. By the way: I am not a master at having everything handled in my life. I screw up *all the time*. I am still late from time to time. I sometimes avoid dealing with tough issues. However, I am *aware* and *clear* that I am doing this to myself.

If we can't honor our time commitments, what can we honor?

When I go to clean something up with someone, I don't add an excuse or justification. I simply say, "I am so sorry that I am late. I said that I would meet you at 3:00 p.m., and I was late. My promise is to be on time." That's it. I don't add any more. I just "be responsible" for the fact that I was late and I did not keep my promise.

The same is true if I promised someone an email, or some other piece of information. I simply call or write them with the information that I said I would, and an apology for not doing what I said I would by when I said I was going to do it. That restores my integrity with that person.

Does the fact that I apologized make it right? Will that other person still be mad at me, or hold it against me? Possibly. If I am constantly not doing what I said I was going to do, then yes, that person is not going to trust me or believe anything that comes out of my mouth.

My kids know that I take door knocking and exercising seriously. They also know that I will always be there to pick them up—on time. It is extremely rare that I am late picking them up from scheduled activities. However, I am often late in leaving on time for a "casual" appointment. For example, if we are going to Costco, I will often be the last one ready. I tell everyone that we are leaving at 1:00 p.m., and then at 1:07 I am filling my water bottle or making a cup of coffee to go. Even when I leave on time, the kids only remember all the times that I was "late."

I am not perfect, and nor will I ever be. I might never be late again leaving the house. Yet it will take them a long time to forget all the times I was late. I, not them, will have to demonstrate that I am on time. What's the point here? Twofold: (1) Whatever pattern of behavior we set is not only hard to break, but it takes time; (2) It's up to us. I can't blame the kids or anyone or anything else. I am the one that was late and set the pattern.

There's Nobody to Blame

Which brings me, ultimately, to my favorite distinction: responsibility. Let me say again that I am not perfect. I screw up all the time. I am about to talk about responsibility, and there are many, many times where I have not been responsible. On the other hand, it is something that I take seriously and that has made the most significant impact on the overall quality of my life.

When I was doing that leadership course in the middle of 2000, one Friday night class gave me something that altered my life forever. The two men leading that evening were Perry and Terry. I don't remember the entire discussion that night, but at one point we were talking about responsibility and relationships. Perry went on to say that whenever his marriage wasn't working, he knew right where to look: himself (with a big thumb pointing back at him). No matter what, no matter the circumstance. Even if his partner was a little responsible, or he felt it was all his partner, no matter what, the place to look was always within himself.

Right then, as I was listening to him I thought, "Yeah, but what about those times where my wife *really* had a lot to do with it?" Even those times. Every moment in life where something wasn't working, what if I could come from the point of view that I was 100% responsible? One-hundred percent. All the time. No matter what! To many people, this concept seems crazy and impossible to implement.

Now—you've really got to get this—to be 100% responsible is not to be at blame or fault!!! Let me say that again, because you probably didn't get what I said: Responsibility is **not** the same as blame or fault. Those are different things.

What I am saying here is that "being responsible" is a choice, a point of view that we can CHOOSE, that gives us power and access to a life that works.

Because the moment that we choose to be responsible, we get to be at the source of our life. We get the power.

Why? Because the moment that we choose to be responsible, we get to be at the source of our life. We get the power. We are not the victim of, or at the effect of, anything! This is especially true in our relationships, but it applies in all areas.

Here's an example in my real estate business. By 2019, I had been selling real estate full time for over 14 years. In the middle of that year, a client called and left a very upsetting voicemail. He was frustrated with all the emails he was getting in the middle of his transaction, and he wasn't sure what to sign and why he needed to sign them.

My very first reaction was, "What the heck? You are a savvy professional, you know what these are, what are you getting all upset about?" Then I paused, took a deep breath, and looked at the situation again. I deal with the home-selling process every week, every month, year in and year out. How often do my clients? For many of my clients, it's once every 10, 20, or 50 years! This particular client hadn't sold a home in 15 years.

I called him back and said, "I am so sorry. My apologies that these forms were not explained correctly. Would you mind if we went through them now so you can be crystal clear what these all are and why they are important?"

What do you think he said? "Of course! That would be really helpful."

Ten years ago, I am not so sure that I would have called with that response, and 20 years ago—not a chance. I would have called him back, or emailed him, with some snarky response that made him feel like an idiot. I would have shown him why he was stupid and that he should grow up and pay attention. I would have blamed him.

Do I get this right all the time? Absolutely not. But I am aware. I know that any time things are not going well, or there is tension, upset, or something else off in the space, there is something that I can be responsible for.

"I Am Sorry" Creates Space

Blaming is a normal place to go. When we get into a disagreement with someone, or there is something unsettling between two people, it is very normal for us to sit there and ruminate in our head, "It's their fault. They should _____." The blank can be filled in with the action that you believe would rectify the situation. We *all* do this, have done this, and will do this again in the future.

Now, are we committed to being right or are we committed to moving forward? Because if we are committed to being right, we will not be moving forward (most likely). If nothing else, being right creates distance between us and another. In the example of my client, being right could have cost me that relationship. It could have cost me future referrals. Not understanding his point of view, not trying to understand his concerns, *would have made no difference for him . . . or me.*

Ray Dalio, in his book, *Principles,* outlined beautifully what happens when we focus on being right: It means that we are making the other person wrong! If we are always entering a discussion or situation by having to be right, then by definition, we are making that other person wrong. Imagine that we are the other person, how do we feel when someone is making us wrong? How do we feel when someone is blaming us? It feels awful! It puts us on the defensive! It puts on a competitive plane, not a cooperative or collaborative arc. Do we really want to do that to our family and loved ones? Our clients?

As smart as "I think I am," I can also be pretty stubborn and dense. I had heard this concept, in a different context before. Somehow, when I heard Dalio explain it, I heard it in a different way. I thought of all the many years when I was married, and all the times with friends, with family, with work peers—when I "had to be right." It now hit me square in the eyes—focusing on being right was killing my relationships.

What does this look like on the court? I like "I'm sorry." Not the "Oh, sorry" that sometimes we say when we accidentally bump into a stranger in a store. I mean an authentic "I'm sorry for _____," and then filling in the blank with something specific. Consider that there is always something we can be responsible for. Always. We just have to be willing to look. This is a big stretch here. Most people reading this are like, "NO WAY." Fine, you can take that point of view, but is it serving you? Consider that there is always something that we can be responsible for. You would have to give up being "right" and be willing to say, "I'm sorry for . . ."

Being willing to say that we're sorry, with some specificity, gives authenticity to what is being said. The example with my client started with "I'm sorry . . ." It immediately created space for us to have a conversation. Think about the last time that you were in a conversation with an agent on the other side of a transaction. When things aren't going well, what is the typical reaction? We say, "They are an idiot, if they just did ____, this would be fine." Instead, we could *call* them (not text or email), and say, "Hey, it looks like this impasse over the inspection item is causing such a fuss. I'm really sorry that we did not know about the cracked heat exchanger on the furnace beforehand. That probably would have been a lot easier for everyone to deal with." What is the other person going to say? They are going to say, "Yes, that's right." So, instead of arguing why your clients aren't fixing it, or aren't giving you credit, you've acknowledged the issue. You have taken responsibility for the problem.

"I'm sorry" creates an opening. If you authentically mean it and can find something specific to be responsible for, it completely shifts the dynamics of the relationship/conversation. It means being responsible.

Responsibility brings power and freedom; it also leaves us as the source of our life. Being in that place brings peace. It doesn't mean that things will always work out, or that life will always be smooth sailing. It does mean that, regardless of what is happening in our life, we have a place to go in order to move ourselves forward. Ultimately, that is the direction to head: forward.

PROLOGUE

GET GOING

"People who get things done in this
world don't wait for the spirit to move
them; they move the spirit."
— David Schwartz, *The Magic of Thinking Big*

It seems so easy. Get a real estate license, start talking to people, do that every day, and voila! We are now making the six-figure income (or more) that we dreamed about.

As you know, it is not easy, but it *is* simple. It really is about being clear who we are, what we want, why we want it, mapping out a plan and a process, and then going to work. Day in, day out, trying as hard as possible to not let life and circumstances take us off track.

This book was not designed for people who want to grow a big team or even to grow a large, 100-plus transaction business. This is for the people who want a real estate advisory practice, one that serves clients well and gets paid their full fee for doing so. It is intended for the person who calls themselves a professional.

Professionals are responsible. Professionals don't get caught up in the moment. Professionals don't let distractions take them off course—or if they do, they know how to get right back on track again. Professionals don't take things personally. Professionals are not in it for a quick buck, they are in it for the long haul.

The Stoic Seneca said that the Greek word *euthymia* (English translation: tranquility) is "*the sense of our own path and how to stay on it without getting distracted by all the others that instruct it.*"

My journey happened to be at the doors. I suspect yours will be somewhere else, but maybe not. Wherever your journey takes you, it will involve getting knocked off course. It will require you to work, fight, ease, and glide your way back onto course. It will also require you to remember where you are going, because as Seneca also reminds us, "*If one does not know to which port one is sailing, no wind is favorable.*"

In the day of long, multi-page contracts with ever-increasing addendums and forms; new technology platforms and other requirements that are thrust upon us—the business is getting more complicated. I am asserting that the more we can keep it simple, the more success we will have—not just in "results," but in the overall quality of our lives. Our lives are not only about real estate.

The game we outlined in this book is not about beating our competition. It is not about being number one. It is about putting ourselves on a path of constant improvement, like climbing the mountain that has no peak—"we gotta fall in love with the journey."

Finally, as my favorite David Schwartz quote goes, "Action cures fear." We must get going.

Behind every door is some new opportunity.

Doors don't open themselves.

Doors only open when you knock.

ACKNOWLEDGEMENTS

No one does it alone—and definitely not me. As I said in the preface, the first credit belongs to Steve Shull, who has been pushing me almost since the day I got into real estate. Although he can appear tough and gruff, he has a heart of gold and gives all of himself to his clients, including me. If you get anything out of this book, then the first 'thank you' goes to him.

However, I wouldn't have gone into real estate in the first place without the seeds planted by friends, such as Dave McLaughlin and Jon Lash, who showed me what was possible in real estate. My first example of what it meant to be a professional in this business was my one and only real estate agent (until I became one), Judi Irwin—a total class act.

Then there were all the "old-timers" at the Westlake Village Coldwell Banker office, who were always willing to share what they had learned over the years. Specifically, June Murray gave me a gold coin for being new in the business and starting to knock on doors. As an aside, I have never gone to the doors without that gold coin in my pocket. In my early days, I used it as a source of love, courage, and inspiration. I often think about how many times that I would not have made it out of my car door without her support and encouragement.

The constant throughout my real estate career has been all my friends and fellow agents who have been part of Performance Coaching. Some of us go way back, some of us barely know each other except for what gets shared on our calls and in our programs. What I have learned and who I have become is in large part a function of that collective group experience.

In my early days of real estate, Steve had two co-coaches. Fred Wilson was a wealth of insight, and, in 2006, he allowed me to shadow him for the day in La Quinta, California. That day altered the trajectory of my real estate career and I am forever grateful. Steve's other co-coach in those days was Elaine Stucy, who used to fly out every month from Castle Rock, Colorado. Fast forward a few years later, I moved my entire family to Colorado, where in a business about connecting people and property, I knew neither. Elaine and her family were the only people that I knew when I moved to Colorado in late 2008. Next to Steve, Elaine is the single-most important person to help me succeed. Without her love and support I am absolutely sure that I would have quit a long time ago.

There are so many people that I can think to thank over my real estate journey that it would be a whole other book—if you think your name should have been here, then please know that I already got that and have already thanked you in my heart a thousand times.

As for this book . . . well, I could also think of a hundred people who helped make it happen. A good place to start is with all the members of Bob Ord Toastmasters in Denver, who helped develop me as a speaker and encouraged me that I had something worth saying. Specifically, Luis Tavel, for always being there as my friend, as well as supporting me with his photography and videography skills (author photograph credit is his). There are so many Toastmasters and friends who encouraged me and gave me helpful feedback, but Merv Graham was, and still is, the shining example of who I aspire to be: prepared, classy, eloquent, and always a good dose of levity.

When it came down to writing the book, it was Cathy Fyock, my book coach, who confirmed that the kernel of this book was worth developing, and it was her enthusiasm and belief in me that kept me going.

My editorial board of Elaine Stucy, Karina Stevens, Joy Nowakowski, Farrah Brittany, David Goldsmith, Mitchell Ross, and Mackinzie Ross—thank you for filling in the missing pieces. To my partner Christine, and her mother Jan, for being willing to endure my endless grammar and punctuation atrocities in editing the early drafts of this book. Christine deserves an extra level of acknowledgement and appreciation—in addition to everything else that she has done for me and my family, the entire chapter on gratitude wouldn't have been possible without her.

My family is my life support. No way my life works without them, so there's even more Ross's to thank in addition to those already mentioned: Susan, Richard, Lynda, Kevin, Brent, and Karyn. Karyn gets extra credit for putting up with me during my first ten years in real estate.

Finally, thank you to all the people who allowed me to knock on their door over the years. Ultimately, without you, there would have been no journey to document. Whether we spoke for five seconds or 50 minutes, THANK YOU for opening your door to a stranger, who in many cases became your friend.

Would You Mind Sharing?

No one likes leaving reviews, but . . .

Leaving a review and/or rating wherever you bought the book makes a *huge* difference for spreading this message. Since you made it here, would it be completely unreasonable to ask for a kind review? Please visit the website of wherever you bought the book and leave a review.

Get this book for a friend, associate,
or family member!

If you have found this book valuable and know others who would find it useful, would you be opposed to buying them a copy as a gift? Need multiple copies for your team or organization? Special bulk discounts are available! Please email Hello@ DoorsOpenWhenYouKnock.com or call 720-826-8190.

Would You Like Steven to Speak to Your Organization?

Steven Ross is a professional speaker and trainer, committed to making a difference for his audiences. If your group is looking to take more consistent action, create more opportunity, and operate with more freedom, then contact Steven to learn how you can bring his message to your organization, call 720-826-8190 or email Booking@DoorsOpenWhenYouKnock.com.

ABOUT THE AUTHOR

Originally from Southern California, Steven began selling real estate there in 2005, and after moving to Colorado in 2009 built another real estate practice from scratch.

Steven says that he is the "worst type of person to be a real estate agent" because:

* He's an introvert.
* He doesn't work nights or weekends.
* You can't find him online.
* He doesn't do parties or events.
* In fact, he's completely antisocial.

Yet he built a successful real estate business twice by doing one thing and one thing only: knocking on doors—over 125,000 of them.

In addition to selling real estate, Steven has spent the last 20 years studying and helping people move forward in the areas of life that are important to them. As a speaker and trainer, he works with other sales professionals to maximize their time and money, developing a business that gives them more time and freedom.

Steven lives with his family in a suburb of Denver, Colorado.

For more information, go to www.DoorsOpen WhenYouKnock.com.